A WORLD ALIGHT WITH SPLENDOUR

Peter Hannan SJ

A World
Alight with Splendour

OUR HUMAN EXPERIENCE OF THE HOLY SPIRIT

the columba press

First published in 2008 by
the columba press
55A Spruce Avenue, Stillorgan Industrial Park,
Blackrock, Co Dublin

Cover by Bill Bolger
Origination by The Columba Press
Printed in Ireland by ColourBooks Ltd, Dublin

ISBN 978 1 85607 631 9

A note of gratitude

I want to thank all those who have helped me to write this book. I want
to thank my parents and family who have nurtured my faith, the many
Jesuits who over the years have inspired and encouraged me, the members of my community who have generously left me the space to write
and tolerated those 'years and years of world without event' that go
into writing a book. I thank my friends Cora, Patrick and Adrian who
have listened to and been enthusiastic about my meandering thoughts
and enthusiasms as this book developed. Finally, I want to thank
Genevieve who as friend and critic has done much to shape this book.

Table of Contents

Introduction   7

PART ONE

Introduction   11
Chapter 1   The importance of personal experience   13
Chapter 2   Universal Experience   17
Chapter 3   The Christian experience of passionate love   21
Chapter 4   The context of the Song of Songs   27

PART TWO

Introduction   35
Chapter 5   Made in God's image   37
Chapter 6   Love   41
Chapter 7   The growth of interior knowledge   45
Chapter 8   The glory within   49
Chapter 9   Finding glory in each other   53
Chapter 10   The union that glory draws us into   57
Chapter 11   A culture of enjoyment   61

PART THREE

Introduction   65
Chapter 12   Nature of the Spirit as it grew in history   67
Chapter 13   The role of the Spirit within the Trinity   71
Chapter 14   The Spirit leads us into 'all the truth'   75
Chapter 15   How the Spirit leads us into 'all the truth'   79
Chapter 16   Reflection   83
Chapter 17   Prayer as a time to remember   87
Chapter18   Contemplating Jesus in the Gospels   91
Chapter 19   The Mass   95
Chapter 20   The Spirit as our 'Advocate'   99

Chapter 21   The Fellowship of the Spirit   103

PART FOUR

Introduction   107
Chapter 22   Seven Gifts of the Spirit   109
Chapter 23   The Gift of Understanding   113
Chapter 24   The Gift of Wisdom   117
Chapter 25   The Gift of Knowledge   121
Chapter 26   The Gift of Fear   125
Chapter 27   The Gift of Piety   129
Chapter 28   The Gift of Fortitude   133
Chapter 29   The Gift of Counsel   137

PART FIVE

Introduction   141
Chapter 30   Eros   143
Chapter 31   Agape   147
Chapter 32   The love that accepts us as we are   151
Chapter 33   The love that appreciates and delights in us   155
Chapter 34   Provident Love   159
Chapter 35   Personal Love   163
Chapter 36   Passionate Love   167
Chapter 37   Permanent Love   171
Chapter 38   Profound Love   175
Chapter 39   Joyful Love   179

PART SIX

Introduction   183
Chapter 40   A brief history of friendship   185
Chapter 41   Three elements of Christian friendship   189
Chapter 42   The first element of friendship: Benevolence   193
Chapter 43   The second element of friendship:
Mutual sharing   197
Chapter 44   The third element of friendship:
Conversation   201
Chapter 45   The union that friendship creates
and maintains   205

Introduction

As I have struggled over the last four years to write this book about the Holy Spirit, I have had ambivalent feelings about it. At times I feel I am being completely unrealistic in describing the world of our dreams that the Spirit seeks to lead us into. This is the world of God's passionate love and of how its beauty draws us into an intimate relationship with him and into the joy that surrounds this. Over against this ideal world is another that at times seems overwhelmingly real, so that its lack of love, its nastiness, its broken relationships and the sadness of these make the ideal world of God's dream for us seem irrelevant.

In the end, however, the ultimate reality of the good news Jesus asks us to believe in always prevails. This is the world of our deepest dream, a world alight with the splendour of God's love and of the intimacy and joy this love draws us into. It is a world where 'Earth's crammed with heaven, and every bush afire with God'. (E. B. Browning)

It is on the intimate and practical role that the Holy Spirit plays in the realisation of this dream that this book will focus. It will explore this in the context of the passion of the three persons of the Trinity to reveal themselves to us and so to incorporate us into their life. The Spirit's role in this is twofold: to pour the love of God into our hearts and then to lead us step by step into an interior knowledge of the human way Jesus expresses this love. (Rom 5:5, Jn 16:13-15)

Selecting the right image
Having been a teacher for twelve years, I know that we attain an intimate knowledge of anything only if it is explained to us in terms of our own experience. The experience we will use to un-

derstand the gift of love the Holy Spirit gives us and leads us into is the passionate love we experience when we fall in love. The reason for choosing this kind of love is that it seems best suited to illustrate the passionate nature of the Trinity's love for us as well as the passionate nature of their desire to reveal it to us. It also expresses the passionate nature of the response they seek from us when they invite us to receive and return their love with our whole 'heart and soul and mind and strength'.

Our guide into love and relationship
The book then is about how the Spirit guides us on our journey into the love that is at the centre of our dream. It tries to discover how this love and the relationships it creates and sustains develop as we make our way through three ages of love. There is an age when, as children, we experience the love of affection or the acceptance and affirmation of our parents and the sense of personal significance this gives us. We enter the age of passionate love when we take responsibility for loving others as we love ourselves or as Jesus has loved us. What very often brings about this dramatic change from the self-preoccupation of childhood and adolescence to loving others as we do ourselves is that we fall in love. If we learn how to make our relationships not only permanent but also profound and joyful, we enter into the third age of love, that of friendship.

> Theoretically, this transformation of love is quite possible. The day will come when, after harnessing space, the winds, the tides and gravitation, we shall harness for God the energies of love. And, on that day, for the second time in the history of the world, we shall have discovered fire. (Teilhard de Chardin)

The six parts of this book
Part 1 looks at four ways we experience the passionate love of God that the Spirit gives us a gift of and leads us into.

Part 2 explores the dream which the Spirit's love inspires in us; the dream of a love whose splendour draws us into the life of the Trinity and into the joy of this union.

Part 3 contemplates how the Spirit leads us into the love of the Father and Jesus so that we realise their dream for us.

Part 4 examines how, by giving us seven gifts, the Spirit involves every area of our life in the realisation of the Trinity's dream for us.

Part 5 describes various kinds of love the Spirit leads us into as we move through the three ages of love in life: from affection to passionate love and thus to the fulfilment of this in friendship.

Part 6 looks at friendship as the fulfilment of the Christian dream of sharing fully in the life of the Trinity.

Introduction

If we are to understand and appreciate the wondrous nature of what Christians have come to believe about the Holy Spirit, we must look at it from within our personal experience. If we do not, what we believe about the Spirit will not be real for us or engaging. Therefore, to savour something of the mystery of the Spirit's gift of love and how the same Spirit leads us into an interior knowledge of it, we will explore four mutually dependent and enriching experiences we have of passionate love. The reason why we focus on this kind of love is because it best reflects the passion of the Trinity to reveal how passionately they love each of us and how much they want us to abide in their love.

In chapter 1 we will look at our personal experience of falling in love and at the passionate love this leads to. In chapter 2 we will reflect on the universal experience of passionate love that we find expressed in the stories people tell. In chapter 3 we will look at how rooted our experience of passionate love is in the bible experience of God being Love and we his Beloved. Finally, in chapter 4 we will explore the way Christians have striven to knit together these three kinds of experience as they sought to answer the question: What does it mean to be a Christian.

PART 1

Introduction

If we are to understand and appreciate the wondrous nature of what Christians have come to believe about the Holy Spirit, we must look at it from within our personal experience. If we do not, what we believe about the Spirit will not be real for us or engaging. Therefore, to savour something of the mystery of the Spirit's gift of love and how the same Spirit leads us into an interior knowledge of it, we will explore four mutually dependent and enriching experiences we have of passionate love. The reason why we focus on this kind of love is because it best reflects the passion of the Trinity to reveal how passionately they love each of us and how much they want us to abide in their love.

In chapter 1 we will look at our personal experience of falling in love and at the passionate love this leads to. In chapter 2 we will reflect on the universal experience of passionate love that we find expressed in the stories people tell. In chapter 3 we will look at how rooted our experience of passionate love is in the bible experience of God being Lover and we his Beloved. Finally, in chapter 4 we will explore the way Christians have striven to knit together these three kinds of experience as they sought to answer the question, What does it mean to be a Christian?

Four mutually dependent and enriching kinds of experience
of the passionate love of the Trinity
as a context for understanding our belief in the Holy Spirit
so that this becomes more real, engaging and credible:

Our Personal Experience
of falling in love, being in love and remaining in love
and its powerful effect on us

Our Universal Experience
as a traditional wisdom expressed in the stories people tell
allows us to explore our dream through the experience of others

Our Bible Experience
of the passionate God of the Old Covenant
and of how Jesus continues to reveal God's love
and dream for us

Tradition
is a synthesis of these three kinds of experience
as it seeks an interior knowledge
of what it means to be a Christian
in the context of the Song of Songs

'Grace is the dynamic state of being in love with God'.
(B. J. Lonergan)

The importance of personal experience

A young peasant lad was summoned by a great king to come and see him. When he arrived at the palace the king said to him, 'My kingdom is so large I cannot meet all my people and touch their lives as I would want to. My wish is that you would give them an impression of who I am.' As symbols of the new role the youth was to play, the king gave him a sceptre, a robe and a crown. As he did not know the king, the poor lad was very confused about what he was being sent to do. He was too awe-struck to ask the king so he went to consult a wise man. He was told by him to go back to his little farm and just be himself. As time went, on more and more people came to visit him for they found in him a sympathetic ear and a compassionate heart. Gradually he realised that this was what the Great King had sent him to do. This was the way he was to give people an impression of what the Great King was like.

The impression of love that the important people in our lives give us is worth remembering and making our own of, as it gives us a very valuable insight into what God's love is like. For example, the love of a friend can open our heart to some aspect of love and, as a result, God can then speak to this part of us and be heard because we have some experience of what this love feels like. When the divine love speaks to our personal experiences of human love in this way, the divine love becomes more clearly defined, more colourful and engaging. Thus, God's love can involve our whole person, body and soul, mind and heart and become an experience that engages our whole person.

It is unfortunate that today the world of the Spirit has become so cut off from the world of our personal experience that both suffer as a result. The former becomes less real and relevant while the latter loses much of its meaning and value. We are, therefore, badly in need of a bridge to connect these two worlds if we are to get a picture of the Spirit that engages our whole person, our senses and soul, our mind and heart. However, before we begin to build this bridge we need to outline two aspects of our relationship with the Spirit which we will focus on in this book.

The Spirit pours the love of God into our hearts

The first aspect is based on our belief that the love of God 'has been poured into our hearts' by the Spirit. (Rom 5:5) This love is at the heart of what Karl Rahner calls the most important reality in the whole of the Christian tradition. This is the fact that the three persons of the Trinity are passionate about revealing themselves to us. What they reveal is the passionate love that they are, a love that is revealed to us in each gospel story but especially in the passion and death of Jesus when he loves us 'to the utmost extent'. (Jn 13:1) The Spirit's role in this revelation is to give us an intimate knowledge of this love, its length and breadth, its height and depth.

The Spirit leads us into 'all the truth'

In the second aspect of our relationship with the Spirit we focus on how the Spirit leads us into 'all the truth' or into this interior knowledge of the love of God that Jesus expresses in human terms. (Jn 16:13-15) The Spirit does this by enlightening our minds and attracting our hearts. By enlightening us the Spirit gives us a glimpse of God's love and by attracting us she enables us to respond to the attractiveness or glory inherent in this love by making our own of it. In practice, we learn to be sensitive to this love and to its attractiveness through reflection and to savour and make our own of it through prayer. To facilitate our becoming more sensitive and responsive to this enlightenment and attraction, the Spirit gives us seven gifts called, Wisdom, Understanding, Knowledge, Piety, Counsel, Fortitude and Fear of the Lord.

In search of an image
We now need to ask ourselves the question, What human experience of love would make the magnificent vision of the Spirit's
love most real, colourful, engaging and thus most credible for
us? The one we will use is that which Christians from the 4th to
the 13th century used when they chose, under the Spirit's guidance, to see their lives in terms of the passionate love depicted in
the Song of Songs. This kind of love is, as we have seen, the best
reflection in human terms of the passionate nature of the
Trinity's love which the Spirit gives us as a gift. This is the love
that the Great Commandment urges us to receive and respond
to with a passion or with our whole body and soul, mind and
heart. (Jn 15:9-10, Lk 10:25-28)

An image we may resist
To portray the Christian life in terms of passionate love might
seem to be unrealistic. This may be because people tend to see
passionate love mainly in physical and sexual terms or in terms
of the strong feelings they experience when they first fall in love.
It may thus be considered unrealistic to expect that this would
continue as a relationship matures. Nevertheless, when a man
and a woman fall in love they are drawn into what very often
becomes for them the most important relationship of their lives.
With all its human limitations, it can become for them the relationship which best fulfils the promise it makes to realise their
dream of love and of the intimacy and joy which the inherent attractiveness of this love leads to. There is a path this love would
lead them along if they are willing to move from falling in love
to being in love and thence to remaining in love. The path love
would have them follow is something like the following:

Falling in love
At the first stage of falling in love the boy and the girl find their
lives beginning to centre on each other. They each want to know
as much as they can about the other and, as they do, they gradually become conscious of ways in which they concur in their
ways of seeing, feeling and acting but also of ways in which
they differ. They want to change what prevents them from fitting in with each other and so they want to find out all they can

about each other, to know whether their love is strong enough to overcome their differences. They ask themselves if they really love each other sufficiently to leave everything to be together. Eventually, they are ready to commit themselves to share their lives together.

The effects of being in love

There are a number of interesting characteristics that are distinctive to falling in love and that give people that are in love the energy they need to bring their relationship to fruition. For example, there is an *intensity* about it in that people who fall in love find each other intensely attractive or beautiful. This may not be obvious to those outside the relationship so that people may say, 'I do not know what she finds in him.' We speak about them as being enamoured, enraptured, and enthralled by each other, which highlights the beauty or radiance they find in each other.

Another characteristic is that the two people in love become the centre of each other's world. They want to be together and to become united in mind and heart. Whereas before they met, their lives, especially as adolescents, centred on themselves, now they *begin to make the other the centre of their attention and concern.* They are led into loving the other person as they do themselves. We notice also that when people are in love they become *wholly involved* in their relationship; their senses, as well as their soul, heart and mind get caught up in it. As the intense attractiveness moves from what they see with their senses to what their minds are convinced of, their union becomes stronger. Another noticeable effect of being in love is the *joy* two people experience in being together. They experience joy at a physical and emotional level and even more so in the glimpses they get of each other's love. The deepest kind of joy is experienced when these glimpses are dwelt with and become convictions of being loved.

However, the most remarkable characteristic of passionate love is *the transforming effect* it has on the two people who are in love. It becomes a catalyst for the radical change that occurs when their falling in love eventually becomes a remaining in love. For this to happen their love must be made to last and to deepen so that their passionate love finds fulfilment in friendship.

CHAPTER 2

Universal Experience

Besides our personal experience, there is a more extensive and well-tried wisdom available to us that is called universal experience. The main expression of this is found in the traditional wisdom which we learn from life. For example, each of us inherits a wisdom handed down to us initially by our families but then by our local community, our country, our culture and in the form of religious belief. The most popular channel for this wisdom is a story but it also comes in the form of poetry, proverb and song.

A story provides us with an engaging way of reflecting on our experience. Each of us comes to a story with a unique way of seeing things and of evaluating them and each of us hears something significant from a story if we are ready to hear it. The sign that a story has something to say to us is the strong feeling we experience while listening to it.

We have an example of this in the film *Behind the Sun* which tells the story of a boy who lives on a farm. Two things dominate his life: one is the grinding labour from dawn to dusk and the other is a feud between his family and a family who live on a neighbouring farm. One day a woman from a travelling circus gives the boy a book of stories. He becomes intrigued by one of these about a mermaid who lives beside the ocean and he believes she is calling him to join her so that they can live together a life of bliss. From time to time, when he gets a break from the work on the farm, he sits under a tree some distance from his home and enters into an enchanting world of love, intimacy and joy as he remembers the story of the mermaid. In this way he creates for himself a place to dream so that he can survive in the hostile environment he is forced to live in.

Joseph Campbell spent his life studying stories like this that people tell. In his book, *The Hero With A Thousand Faces* he explores his belief that all these stories are about the inner journey we are each called to undertake. In a central chapter entitled, *Atonement With The Father* he explores the idea that our inner journey is basically in search of reconciliation with the father-mother god whose Grace and Mercy draws us into a union and a state of bliss. In other words, the object of our inner journey is the realisation of our dream of love and the intimacy and joy that the intensity of this love draws us into.

> Stories are medicine ... They have such power; they do not require that we do, be or act – we need only listen. The reclamation of any lost psychic drive is contained in stories. *(C. P. Estes)*

Giving ourselves permission to dream
Stories provide us with a chance to dream, permitting us to be in the inner world of relationships and of the love that sustains these. Judged by the standards of our outer world, which focuses on what we *have* and what we *do*, being in our inner world is not a priority and seems an unreal and irrelevant place to be. As a result, we get out of touch with what is important when what is urgent rules our day. In this environment stories, whether we find them in plays, novels or films, provide a 'permissible' way to be in our inner world. This is the world the Great Commandment invites us to be involved in, one where we get our whole person involved in the love we receive and return within the main relationships of our lives. It is in this world that Jesus tells us we will find life in all its fullness. (Lk 10:25-29) Therefore, it is important that we make space to be in this inner world, that we allow ourselves to go bear hunting.

Going Bear-hunting
There was this sociologist who was making a study of some North American Indians. One day she was present when a gov-ernment official was lecturing in a particu-lar village on the necessity of digging proper latrines. The sociologist noticed that one of the Indians burst out laughing at a very boring part of the lecture. She was curi-

ous about this so when the official had gone she asked the Indian what had been so amusing. He said, 'Oh, the bear had just fallen into the water.' When she enquired further she found that every time he became bored, especially during talks from government officials, he would, in his imagination, go bear hunting, and enjoy all the fun and excitement of it.

Stories engage our whole person

During my years as a teacher I became aware of the importance of getting those I taught to enter their inner world by means of stories. I realised the power a story or an image has to arouse our inner wisdom. This is because stories, images and symbols capture the things that are most important for us, the stuff of our dreams of love and intimacy and joy, more effectively than do ideas and facts. Where ideas and facts appeal to our minds, stories and images appeal to our whole person.

There are four ways stories can exercise this appeal. They begin by engaging us at a sensate level as our attention is caught when we listen to what happens in a story. We know from how we are being moved at a feeling level when a story is saying something significant to us at an intuitive level. These glimpses, once aroused and appreciated, can put us in touch with a body of convictions about what is true and worthwhile. These convictions or the vision and values that we have formed throughout our lives are part of an inner wisdom that is largely dormant. Stories help us to arouse and to reflect on this body of inner wisdom. However, getting at this wisdom has a price for it asks us to follow the wisdom of the railway crossing: to stop, to look and to listen.

> What is the price of experience? do men buy it for a song?
> or wisdom for a dance in the street? no, it is bought with
> the price of all that a man hath. (William Blake)

If a story is to reveal its wisdom to us and to speak to our own story, we must be willing to make space for this to happen. We will know when a story asks us to make this space by the strength of the feeling it arouses. It is then up to us to dwell with this moment of enlightenment which the story offers, for it is in savouring and appropriating this that stories nourish us. 'By being the curator of our images we care for our soul'. (St Thomas Moore)

Susan Hill in her novel *Air and Angels* tells a story that can put us in touch with our dream in a deeply affecting way. Read the following brief account of it and notice what it says to you and how you feel about this.

It is the story of Thomas, a young lecturer in Cambridge University and of Kitty a girl aged 16. Early in the novel they spent three days together and even though nothing improper happened between them it was seen to have and so Thomas lost his position and his reputation.

At the end of the book Kitty reflects on the influence of those three days on her life … 'She felt that a hundred, or a thousand years, had passed in three days and that she was grown up and completely adult. It was as if she understood the meaning of all things, had seen to the heart of them and above all understood instinctively that she had known love of a kind she would never know again for the rest of her life. She was humbled by it and grateful for it and ashamed of nothing.'

For Thomas, the memory of his short-lived relationship with Kitty, remained with him for the rest of his life … 'He felt that Kitty was always with him, the memory of her never dimmed or became cloudy and the love he had felt he continued to feel and it was never supplanted. He regretted nothing at all. He had known a brief time of joy, absolute and unalloyed, and saw it as a foretaste of paradise. Many years later, as an old man, standing in the sunshine by the river and seeing a girl in a pale dress on the stone bridge, the past raced towards him, broke over him and became the present. He felt anew what he had felt during those three days, love, fresh and raw and vivid. Love, he had never forgotten for one second of a lifetime since, or never once regretted.'

CHAPTER 3

The Christian experience of passionate love

Into Great Silence is a film about the lives of the monks of Le Grand Chartreuse, one of the most famous monasteries in Europe. As we view the stark simplicity of their lives we ask ourselves, Why do they live like this and what keeps them going? Why do they come and why do they stay? An answer to these questions is suggested in a passage from scripture that often appears on the screen. This is a verse from the prophet Jeremiah: 'You have seduced me, Yahweh, and I have let myself be seduced.' (Jer 20:7) The significance of this seduction is borne out by an incident in Patrick Leigh Fermor's book, *A Time to Keep Silence* in which he describes his experiences of visiting six very famous European monasteries. In one of these, curious to find out what drew the monks to their unusual way of life, he says:

'I asked one of the monks how he could sum up, in a couple of words, his way of life. He paused a moment and said, "Have you ever been in love?" I said, "Yes." A large Fernandel smile spread across his face, "Good", he said, "It is an exact parallel".'

The Old Covenant image of God as passionate lover

In the Old Testament God is revealed as one who seduces us or wins our hearts by the attractiveness of his love. He lures us out into the desert and speaks to our heart. 'Therefore, I will now allure her and bring her into the wilderness, and speak tenderly to her ... And I will take you for my wife forever; I will take you for my wife in righteousness and in justice, in steadfast love, and in mercy. I will take you for my wife in faithfulness; and you shall know the Lord.' (Hos 2:14, 19-20)

A love built on affection
The tenderness of God's passionate love for us is movingly expressed in Jeremiah. 'I have loved you with an everlasting love and I am constant in my affection for you.' (Jer 31:3) Hosea also describes God lavishing an affectionate love on us, a love that accepts our waywardness, delights in us and remains deeply concerned for our welfare. 'When Israel was a child, I loved him, and out of Egypt I called my son. The more I called them, the more they went from me; they kept sacrificing to the Baals, and offering incense to idols. Yet it was I who taught Ephraim to walk, I took them up in my arms; but they did not know that I healed them. I led them with cords of human kindness, with bands of love. I was to them like those who lift infants to their cheeks. I bent down to them and fed them.' (Hos 11:1-4)

A love that clothes us with splendour
When we are in love with someone we find beauty in the one we love. Ezekiel highlights the fact that God in his passionate love for his beloved bestows his own splendour on her. 'I clothed you with embroidered cloth and with sandals of fine leather; I bound you in fine linen and covered you with rich fabric. I adorned you with ornaments: I put bracelets on your arms, a chain on your neck, a ring on your nose, earrings in your ears, and a beautiful crown upon your head. You were adorned with gold and silver, while your clothing was of fine linen, rich fabric, and embroidered cloth. You had choice flour and honey and oil for food. You grew exceedingly beautiful, fit to be a queen. Your fame spread among the nations on account of your beauty, for it was perfect because of my splendour that I had bestowed on you, says the Lord God.' (Ezk 16:9-14)

The joy of being so loved
Isaiah highlights the glory God's passionate love bestows on us and the delight God as the bridegroom takes in us his bride. 'The nations shall see your vindication, and all the kings your glory; and you shall be called by a new name that the mouth of the Lord will give. You shall be a crown of beauty in the hand of the Lord, and a royal diadem in the hand of your God. You shall no more be termed Forsaken, and your land shall no more be

22

termed Desolate; but you shall be called My Delight Is in Her, and your land Married; for the Lord delights in you, and your land shall be married. For as a young man marries a young woman, so shall your builder marry you, and as the bridegroom rejoices over the bride, so shall your God rejoice over you.' (Is 62:2-5)

These passages from the Old Testament reveal God's love in terms of the passionate love of a man for a woman, of a bridegroom for his bride, of a husband for his wife. The intense attractiveness or glory this love finds in the beloved, and the intimacy and joy this draws us into, is what we are made for, the dream we seek to realise in all our relationships.

Interpreting the gospels in terms of passionate love

In the gospels Jesus continues to reveal himself in terms of passionate love. The way it develops is similar to the way we saw the passionate love of a man and a woman developing in Chapter 1.

With the words, 'Come and see' Jesus invites his first disciples to come to know him. (Jn 1:39) As they do so they are so deeply affected by the experience that they 'leave everything and follow him'. This has all the marks of a falling in love experience, of a passionate love whose magnetic power draws them to centre their lives on Jesus.

There follows a period when his disciples come to know Jesus intimately and are drawn into a personal relationship with him. He becomes increasingly attractive for them as they 'see his glory' or the radiance of his love and so learn to believe in him. (Jn 2:11) This period ends with Jesus asking them, 'Who do you say that I am?' and their expression of tentative belief that he is the Messiah. (Lk 9:18-20)

On their admission of this, Jesus begins to challenge them with changing their minds and hearts in order that they might accept the kind of Messiah he is destined to be. This radical change of mind and heart is necessary if they want to remain with him on his journey towards his death in Jerusalem.

During the next period the disciples struggle to come to know Jesus under his new guise as the one who will suffer and die for love of them. They need to know more about him if they are to decide he is the one whom they are willing to commit themselves to as their Saviour and Lord.

It is in the light of his death and resurrection that they finally decide to centre their lives on him. This is their final leap of faith in the reality that he is their Lord, the Messiah who is the fulfilment of all their hopes.

In the Acts of the Apostles we see how the disciples have committed themselves completely to making Jesus the Lord of their lives. 'Therefore let the entire house of Israel know with certainty that God has made him both Lord and Messiah, this Jesus whom you crucified.' (Acts 2:36) Paul in his letter to the Christians at Philippi describes his relationship with Jesus in terms of his constant effort to 'take hold of' Jesus in the same way as Jesus 'took hold of' him. 'Not that I have secured it already, nor yet reached my goal, but I am still pursuing it in the attempt to take hold of the prize for which Christ Jesus took hold of me.' (Phil 3:12)

The effect of Jesus' passionate love on us

As we saw in chapter 1, falling in love has a dramatic effect on us in the way it arouses our dream of a love whose intense attractiveness draws us into an intimate relationship with the one we love and into the joy of this. We will conclude this chapter by looking at the effects of Jesus' passionate love on us, of his 'taking hold of', seizing, taking possession of and enrapturing us as he did Paul. We will look at how God in Jesus reveals to us a love whose intense attractiveness or glory draws us into a share of their own union and into all the joy of this. This is the ultimate realisation of our dream described for us in Jn 14-17.

The passionate nature of Jesus' love ...

John describes the love Jesus has for us as a love 'to the utmost extent' (Jn 13:1) and Jesus calls it the greatest the world has ever known. (Jn 15:13) It is so passionate, permanent and profound that it is no less than a share in the love that Jesus has for his Father and that his Father has for him. (Jn 14:21, 17:23) It is the love the Spirit personifies, gives us a gift of (Rom 5:5-11) and leads us into an intimate knowledge of. (Jn 16:13-15) The result is that we experience it from within the Trinity and can say with Jesus, 'Abba! Father!' (Rom 8:14-17)

... radiates a beauty ...

There is a glory, radiance, beauty or splendour about all love but especially about the passionate love of Jesus revealed in his death and resurrection. This love is uniquely glorious in that it is the climax of the revelation of his love and what he calls his 'hour of glory'. It is in this event that the Father desires to reveal the radiant glory of Jesus to us (Jn 16:14, 33) so that we might see the Father's glory in the human way Jesus expresses it. (Jn 14:9-11, 13) It is this divine glory that Jesus wants to share with us when he says, 'The glory that you have given me I have given to them.' (Jn 17:22) It is through the Holy Spirit that we are given an intimate knowledge of this glory and of how we share in its 'ever-increasing splendour'. (2 Cor 3:18, Rom 8:17)

... that draws us towards 'complete' union with him ...

As the first disciples of Jesus came to know him they were so overawed by the attractiveness of his love that 'they left everything and followed him'. (Lk 5:11) The radiance of Jesus' love, if we get to know it, draws us too to become his followers and eventually into the 'complete' union which the Father and Jesus enjoy. 'That they may be one, as we are one, I in them and you in me, that they may become completely one'. (Jn 17:22-23) This union is the realisation of Jesus' plan that we should be as intimate with him as he and his Father are with each other. (Jn 14:3, 10-11) Jesus wants us to be as close to him as the branches are to the vine whose life they share. (Jn 15:1-6, 15) The Spirit leads us into this divine union just as she leads us into the love that creates and sustains it. (Jn 16:13-15) In this union that the Spirit brings about we become one with Jesus before the Father and as a result we can say with him, 'Abba Father!' (Rom 8:14-17)

... at the core of which is an all-pervasive joy ...

Jesus promises us that if we 'abide in' his love and become one in mind and heart with him, we will share in his joy, a joy that is 'complete'. (Jn 15:9-11) This joy grows according as we learn to believe that we are loved by Jesus just as he is loved by his Father; our joy is always proportionate to our faith. Since no human being can give us such joy it is Jesus' special gift to us, (Jn 14:27) a gift no one can take away from us. (Jn 16:21-22) Peace and joy are the 'fruit of the Spirit', an unfolding of her love and a distinctive mark of the Christian community that the Spirit's love creates. (Gal 5:23, Rom 14:17)

The magnetic pull of Jesus' glory creates a new order or union
As John reflects on this final period of Jesus' life he is conscious of the power of the beauty of Jesus' love over him. He is conscious too of how the ultimate beauty of Jesus, being lifted up on the cross and in the glory of his resurrection, draws all to him as the magnetic centre of life. (Jn 12:32) He sees, in the incident where it is reported that the whole world is running after Jesus, a symbol of how Jesus can engage our whole person in this magnetic pull he exerts on us. (Jn 12:19) Thus, Jesus, in drawing us to himself, reintegrates all that is within us and all that is without, gathering 'into one the dispersed children of God'. (Jn 11:52)

CHAPTER 4

Seeing our lives
in the context of the Song of Songs

A film called *The Bridges of Madison County* tells the story of Francesca, of her love for Robert her husband and for their two children. Once, when she was alone for a week while her husband and children had gone to a state fair, she met Richard who was photographing the bridges of Madison County for *The National Geographic* magazine. Over the five days they spent together a relationship developed between them that changed their lives. They experienced three interrelated levels of being in love. At the first level they experienced a deep sexual attraction for each other and the times of intimate union this led to became part of the second level. At this second level their experience led them to question and clarify how they felt about what was happening between them. They discussed how they saw themselves as man and woman, how their hopes and dreams had or had not been fulfilled and what they should do in the future. In the end, Francesca decided to remain with her husband and Richard, out of deference to her decision, never contacted her again. Yet, they always remained present to each other. They were both profoundly changed by their experience and entered the third level of their love for each other when they became as 'two spirits in one body'. (Aristotle) At the end of her life Francesca describes how both of them saw their relationship:

'Though we never spoke again to one another we remained bound together as tightly as is possible for two people to be bound. I cannot find the words to express this adequately. He said it best when he told me we had ceased being two separate beings and instead had become a third being formed by the two of us. Neither of us existed independently of that being. And that being was left to wander.'

I have thought a lot about why I have been so moved by this story. I think it is because it provides an analogue for the relationship God wants us to enter into with him and it also gives us a glimpse of the relationship between Jesus and his Father from which the Spirit proceeds. This is the 'fellowship of the Spirit' we are invited into and in which passionate love finds its dream fully realised. Perhaps the reason why *The Bridges of Madison County* is so engaging is that it is a modern rendering of the Song of Songs.

The Song of Songs

In the early centuries of the church when Christians reflected on their experience of Jesus they sought an answer to the question, *What does it mean to be a Christian?* They sought an answer to this not by analysing their experience for its meaning but by choosing an image or symbol that would capture their experience of Jesus 'taking hold of' or enrapturing them. One of the symbols they chose was the *Song of Songs*. Very influential in their choice was chapter 5 of Paul's letter to the Ephesians. There Paul, reflecting on the passionate love of a man and woman in marriage, its splendour and the union it draws them into, compares this with the splendour of Jesus' love of us and with the union this draws us into. Both relationships are enriched by the comparison, especially the relationship between the man and the woman in marriage. This relationship became a 'sacrament' or outward sign of an inward grace in that marriage points beyond itself to the passionate relationship between Jesus and the Christian. It is a passionate love we are made for and is ultimately found in Jesus' love of us 'to the utmost extent'. (Jn 13:1)

It is in the light of this mutually enriching comparison that Hans Urs van Balthasar, perhaps the greatest theologian of the 20th century, believes the Song gained its true significance and its position in the Bible. In his book on the Old Covenant he writes of the Song:

> This loose handful of songs celebrates but one thing: the beautiful, resplendent and awesome glory of the eros between man and woman. Eros' only purpose is loving and being loved. It is the sense-related and intoxicated condi-

tion whereby two persons exist for one another and with one another. Everything is drawn into this whirl of love. Everyone and everything else are seen as extras. There is no historical memory, no mention of God so that it was only an allegorical interpretation that made the book acceptable. Then in this guise it began its triumphant march through the Fathers, the Middle Ages down to the Baroque era.

Up to the 13th century the monasteries of Europe had an important role in shaping the vision and values of Christians. It is an intriguing fact that those who developed the spiritual vision distinctive of monastic life gave a key role to the Song, making it central to the way they saw and lived their lives. In other words, as Balthasar holds, they saw their lives in the context of the Song. It was in it that they found an answer to the question, What does it mean to be a Christian?

The passionate pursuit of a dream

The influence that the Song continues to exert over successive generations of Christians is due to the way it expresses our longing for love and the intimate relationships that love leads us into. This hunger for love underlies all our relationships as it has its roots in the image of God in which we are made. The potential for a God-like love which this gives us is clarified by the Great Commandment which calls us to invest all our resources of body and soul, of mind and heart in receiving and returning love within life's main relationships. It is in this context that we can best appreciate the perennial appeal of the Song as an imaginative expression of our deepest aspirations or of our dream. It is in Jesus that the ideal of the Song becomes a practical reality for us as we come to know his love and ultimately fulfil the dream portrayed so colourfully in the Song.

'I sought him whom my soul loves'

The first element of our dream the Song depicts for us is the love central to it. This love is both longing and delight. The woman in the Song longs to find the one she loves and when she does she delights in his presence. However, she has to live with the reality that sometimes she fails to find him or loses him again when she does find him. 'Upon my bed at night I sought him whom my soul loves; I sought him, but found him not; I called him, but he gave no answer. ... I will seek him whom my soul loves. I sought him, but found him not. "Have you seen him whom my soul loves?" Scarcely had I passed them, when I found him whom my soul loves. I held him, and would not let him go until I brought him into my mother's house, and into the chamber of her that conceived me.' (3:1-4)

'How beautiful you are, my love, how very beautiful'
A feature of the passionate love the Song paints for us is the beauty that the lovers find in each other. The woman finds that the man's love gives her a sense of significance beyond what she has in her family. (1:5-8) She hears him saying how delightful or beautiful she is for him, that she is 'the loveliest of women'. 'How beautiful you are my love, how beautiful you are! Your eyes are doves. How beautiful you are, my Beloved, and how delightful.' (1:15-16) 'Let me see your face, let me hear your voice; for your voice is sweet, and your face is lovely.' (2:14) 'How beautiful you are, my love, how very beautiful!' ... You are altogether beautiful, my love; there is no flaw in you.' (4:1,7)

For the woman too the man's beauty is obvious. 'His appearance is like Lebanon, choice as the cedars. His speech is most sweet, and he is altogether desirable. This is my beloved and this is my friend.' (5:15-16)

'I am my beloved's and my beloved is mine'
The intense attractiveness of the beauty they find in each other draws them into intimacy or into the third element of the dream the man and woman seek to realise. This intimacy is described in a simple and profound way that epitomises the new covenant revealed to Jeremiah when God says that we will be his people and he will be our God. (Jer 31:31-34) 'My beloved is mine and I am his.' (2:16) 'I am my beloved's and my beloved is mine.' (6:3)

'The time of singing has come'
The fourth element of their dream is the joy they experience in each other's company. 'My beloved speaks and says to me: "Arise, my love, my fair one, and come away; for now the winter

is past, the rain is over and gone. The flowers appear on the earth; the time of singing has come".' (2:10-12) The joy they experience is portrayed as a banquet at which they become 'drunk with love'. 'I come to my garden, my sister, my bride; I gather my myrrh with my spice, I eat my honeycomb with my honey, I drink my wine with my milk. Eat, friends, drink, and be drunk with love.' (5:1)

How involved do we wish to get?

In the Song there is a sense of deference for human freedom, an acceptance of human frailty, a respect for what we are willing and for what we are ripe to accomplish. While we are responsible for realising our dream we must not 'awaken love until it is ready'. 'I adjure you, O daughters of Jerusalem, by the gazelles or the wild does: do not stir up or awaken love until it is ready!' (2:7) The Song teaches us that life is all about our relationships and the love that is central to them. However, it believes that these relationships need to be cultivated in a resourceful way if we are to get our whole person engaged in pursuit of the love we receive and return within them. We need to draw on the resources we have in our memory and even more so in our imagination. The Song asks us how much of the passion for love and relationships, that the Great Commandment calls for, do we wish to bring to our quest to realise our dream. The Song depicts a level of involvement that reflects that of Jesus when he asks us to 'abide in' his love by immersing our whole person, body and soul, heart and mind in it. (Jn 15:9-10)

We need our body to communicate

The Song seeks to engage what the Great Commandment calls our 'whole strength' or what we term our body with all its senses. The Song assumes the importance of the body in our relationships and it takes a profound delight in it. The body is relished and praised throughout the book. The Song takes the needs of the body and of the sexual self seriously and also the fact that these are part of more pressing needs. Therefore, the Song often turns back from the physical consummation of love to give a deeper dimension of it space to grow. It is assumed that the body has the power to go beyond the physical, to enter the deeper dimensions of receiving and returning love.

The tendency to overstress the mystical dimension of the Song can diminish its sense of celebration of the beauty of the human body and especially its sexuality. Christians have found this kind of luxuriating in the sexual unreal and even embarrassing and in the other books of the Bible the body is often seen as problematic and as a source of temptation. As a result, we may find it hard to see what corresponds to the following in our relationship with Jesus: 'You have ravished my heart, my sister, my bride, you have ravished my heart with a glance of your eyes, with one jewel of your necklace. How sweet is your love, my sister, my bride! How much better is your love than wine, and the fragrance of your oils than any spice! Your lips distil nectar, my bride; honey and milk are under your tongue; the scent of your garments is like the scent of Lebanon. (4:9-11)

The contribution of feelings to intimacy

The Song engages our 'whole heart' or our feelings in the relationship between the woman and her beloved. Though we may identify with her passionate longing we may resist the way it is so graphically expressed. She does not repress her feelings but is assertive, uninhibited and unabashed about her sexual desires, seeing these as an essential part of the love and intimacy she pursues wholeheartedly. 'You are beautiful as Tirzah, my love, comely as Jerusalem, terrible as an army with banners. Turn away your eyes from me, for they overwhelm me!' (6:4-5)

Cultivating glimpses of glory

The Song involves our 'whole soul' in voicing in very imaginative ways the glimpses of her beloved the woman is given. We find these glimpses expressed in the two poems about the man's beauty and three about the woman's that we find in the Song. Around the glimpses he remembers of her, he builds up, with the help of his imagination, an elaborate picture of her beauty. 'My dove, my perfect one, is the only one, the darling of her mother, flawless to her that bore her. The maidens saw her and called her happy; the queens and concubines also, and they praised her. Who is this that looks forth like the dawn, fair as the moon, bright as the sun, terrible as an army with banners?' (6:9-10)

Relationships founded on the rock of conviction
By dwelling on these glimpses of each other's goodness and beauty, they grow in their convictions of what is true and worthwhile about each other. Coming near the end of the Song, love has become 'as strong as death' and they are no longer at a distance from each other as they are at peace in the sureness of each other's love. 'Set me as a seal upon your heart, as a seal upon your arm; for love is strong as death, passion fierce as the grave. Its flashes are flashes of fire, a raging flame. Many waters cannot quench love, neither can floods drown it. If one offered for love all the wealth of one's house, it would be utterly scorned ... then I was in his eyes as one who brings peace.' (8:6-7, 9)

Thus we see his and her 'whole mind' becoming involved in expressing the lessons they have learned about love along the way, the wisdom love has taught them. For example, there is a balance to be kept between love as delight and love as desire, between resting in and longing for each other's love. The Song asks us to respect the seasons of love, how love comes to us in times of light and in times of darkness, in times of joy and in times of sorrow, in times of adversity and in times of peace.

The importance of the Song
Since I first heard of how important the Song was to western monasticism, I have been intrigued and often wondered why it became such an important part of Christian tradition. Is it that in its description of the passionate love between the man and the woman it helped the men and women of the monastic tradition to understand the love at the core of their relationship with Jesus and to get their whole person involved in this?

Though the Song is no longer central to the way Christians see themselves today, it is still one of the most powerful images of how the intense attractiveness of Jesus' love draws our whole person into an intimate relationship with him. The Song speaks to us in an unrivalled way about the passionate nature of God's love and the passionate response this calls for. It asks us how involved we want to be in our relationship with Jesus, how much of our body and soul, our mind and heart we want to immerse in his love.

PART TWO

Introduction

The intense love between two people who are obviously in love is a sign of a much deeper and more fundamental passionate love. This is a love for which we are all made and that only God can satisfy. It is the object of our deepest dream and of our Grail quest. This dream has its source in the image of God in which we are made and when the love of God is poured into our hearts by the Holy Spirit all the potential of our dream can be realised. It becomes possible to enter into the love of God and all its splendour and so to be drawn into a union with God and into all its joy. Yet in spite of the attractiveness of this our deepest dream, more superficial dreams easily capture our attention with their offer of instant satisfaction. As a result, our deep dream goes underground or becomes dormant and we become like sleepwalkers. Our purpose in the second part of this book is to arouse and clarify our dream and, under the guidance of the Spirit, to see how we can take responsibility for realising it.

The chapters of Part 2 begin by focusing on the source of our dream, the image of God in which we are made. We then look at the love at the core of our dream and at aspects or faces of this love of which the Spirit wants to give us an interior knowledge. Following this we reflect on the intense attractiveness, beauty or glory essential to all love but especially to the love of Jesus that the Spirit leads us into. It is a glory Jesus shares with us and that the Spirit leads us to find in everyone we meet. The final chapters consider how we are drawn into intimacy or union with Jesus, a union permeated by a complete and constant joy.

Four elements of our dream

The dream which God has for us
has its source in the image of God in which we are made

We become capable of a God-like *love*

that radiates a *glory* or beauty

and draws us into a *union* or fellowship
that the three persons of the Trinity want to share with us

this union is an environment where *joy* prevails
a culture of enjoyment or consolation

CHAPTER 5

Made in God's image

There is a significant scene in the film, *Dead Poets' Society* in which Mr Keating, an English teacher in a prestigious school, invites his pupils into the school quadrangle. There he asks three of them to stroll around in a way that will express their own personality. They do this for a short while and then they fall in behind each other and begin to march to the time being beaten out by the rest of the class. Mr Keating, trying to help them understand why they are doing this, says, 'We all have a great need for acceptance but you must trust that your own beliefs are unique even though others may say they are odd or unpopular, even though the herd may go.' 'That's bad.'

Two kinds of tradition
Dead Poets' Society is about two kinds of tradition. One of these, that imposes standards of achievement that are not true to our deeper selves, is deadening in that it kills off the poet in us. The other is enlivening for it fosters a sense of the importance of each person's unique potential. It respects the dream God plants in our heart when he makes us in his own image, a dream we must hold fast to.

> Hold fast to dreams, for if dreams die,
> Life is a broken-winged bird that cannot fly;
> Hold fast to dreams, for when dreams go,
> Life is a barren field, frozen with snow.

We are made in God's image and likeness
The source of our dream is our being made in the image of God. As such we are endowed with intellect and will or with the capacity to receive and respond to the God-like love we long for and that God wants to reveal to us.

> Then God said, 'Let us make humankind in our image, according to our likeness' ... So God created humankind in his image, in the image of God he created them; male and female he created them. God blessed them, and God said to them, 'Be fruitful and multiply, and fill the earth and subdue it.' (Gen 1:26-28)

Being made in God's image we are endowed with the capacity to listen to God's self-revelation as love and with the capacity to appropriate and believe in this revelation.

Crowned with glory and beauty

Because we are made for God's love, we *are* a hunger for it. As a result, when we learn to notice and savour this love, we find it very attractive; we experience its beauty or what is spoken of in the Bible as glory. This glory is found primarily in God but we can also find it in ourselves because God 'has clothed us with his own splendour', (Ezk 16:14) 'crowned us with glory and beauty'.

> When I look at your heavens, the work of your fingers, the moon and the stars that you have established; what are human beings that you are mindful of them, mortals that you care for them? Yet you have made them a little lower than God, and crowned them with glory and beauty.' (Ps 8:3-5)

A beauty that engages our whole person

There has been a tendency to associate our being made in God's image with our spirit as distinct from our body. However, in the Bible, the body is seen as the inseparable companion and revelation of the spirit; it is through the body that we receive love and return it. Because of this close connection, the glory of God once glimpsed engages our whole person and not just our spirit or mind. That we would get our whole person involved in our relationships in this way is the aim of the Great Commandment which invites us to be loved and to love with our body and soul, mind and heart.

> 'Hear, O Israel: The Lord is our God, the Lord alone. You shall love the Lord your God with all your heart, and with all your soul, and with all your might. Keep these words

that I am commanding you today in your heart. (Deut 64-6) 'He endowed them with strength like his own, and made them in his own image ... Discretion and tongue and eyes, ears and a mind for thinking he gave them. He filled them with knowledge and understanding ... And they will praise his holy name, to proclaim the grandeur of his works ... Their eyes saw his glorious majesty, and their ears heard the glory of his voice. (Sir 17:3-13)

The call to intimacy

In the second story of creation in the book of Genesis what is emphasised is the capacity for intimacy that being made in God's image gives us. This capacity for intimacy is exemplified for us by the way the God-like love of the man and the woman for each other draws them into a relationship so intimate that they become 'one body' or one person. For this reason the Bible finds in their relationship the greatest expression of human intimacy and its preferred image of the intimacy or union God seeks to establish with us.

The man gave names to all cattle, and to the birds of the air, and to every animal of the field; but for the man there was not found a helper as his partner. So the Lord God caused a deep sleep to fall upon the man, and he slept; then he took one of his ribs and closed up its place with flesh. And the rib that the Lord God had taken from the man he made into a woman and brought her to the man. Then the man said, 'This at last is bone of my bones and flesh of my flesh; this one shall be called Woman, for out of Man this one was taken.' Therefore a man leaves his father and his mother and clings to his wife, and they become one flesh. And the man and his wife were both naked, and were not ashamed.' (Gen 2:20-25)

As we have already seen, love, beauty and intimacy are an essential part of our being made in the likeness of God. Now, because love is primarily delight, and beauty is what enraptures us, the intimacy these draw us into is a union permeated with joy.

'You shall be called My Delight Is in Her, and your land Married; for the Lord delights in you, and your land shall be married. For as a young man marries a young woman, so shall your builder marry you, and as the bridegroom rejoices over the bride, so shall your God rejoice over you.' (Is 62:4-5)

We find a description of what Jesus sees to be the fulfilment of our dream in chapter 17 of John's gospel. He wants to share with us the exact same love, glory, union and joy that he and his Father share.

I speak these things in the world so that they may have my joy made complete in themselves ... As you, Father, are in me and I am in you, may they also be in us, so that the world may believe that you have sent me. The glory that you have given me I have given them, so that they may be one, as we are one, I in them and you in me, that they may become completely one, so that the world may know that you have sent me and have loved them even as you have loved me. (Jn 17:13, 21-23)

This fulfilment brought about by the Spirit is beyond anything we can imagine.

But, as it is written, 'What no eye has seen, nor ear heard, nor the human heart conceived, what God has prepared for those who love him' these things God has revealed to us through the Spirit; for the Spirit searches everything, even the depths of God.' (1 Cor 2:9)

AN EXERCISE: List the desires that are most pressing for you at this stage of your life. Underline some of these desires that are clearly more important than the others. To become more aware of the relative importance of what you have listed, draw a diagram. The more important desires might be put in an inner circle and the others, according to their importance for you, might be put in other circles further removed from the centre. In the light of what you see to be your dream in life, spend some time in prayer with 1 Kings 3:5-14 and Jn 1:39.

CHAPTER 6

Love

The Fisher King is a film about the search of two men and two women for love. Parry, one of the men, is mad, at least by this world's standards. He is obsessed by the Holy Grail which he believes is in the possession of a millionaire who lives in a castle-like residence. Parry's second obsession is with Lydia, who appears odd in the way she dresses and acts. She is the centre of Parry's day, he follows her to work each morning and is in ecstasy when he catches sight of her.

Joe, the second man, runs a radio programme where people phone in looking for advice. The advice he gives them is neither sensitive nor concerned as his main interest seems to be in scoring points at their expense. Very early in the story Joe realises that Parry's madness is the result of one of his episodes of point scoring. So, driven by guilt he enters Parry's world and gradually grows in understanding of and concern for the realisation of Parry's dream.

By the end of the film it seems that Joe has helped Parry to find the Holy Grail. This is not so much by presenting him with the cup, which for Parry represents the Holy Grail, but by the concern he demonstrates in his efforts to acquire the cup for him. It is not just Parry who has found the Grail. Each of the other three characters in the story also seem to have found it in the give and take of their love for each other. It is as if they have become bound together in a fellowship of concern where each one finds a new and happier life.

The version of the Grail legend told in this film emphasises the importance of the fact that the love of Christ, which the Holy Grail symbolises, often manifests itself through the inconspicuous concern of people for us. As it is revealed in *The Fisher King* it is a concern that is affectionate and passionate as well as profound and joyful and it transforms or brings about a quiet revolution in the lives of the four characters involved.

We find a similar range of ways of loving in how Jesus relates with those he meets in the gospels. These ordinary ways in which he accepts, affirms and makes much of people form the good news that he asks us to 'repent and believe in'. (Mk 1:14-15) We are called to believe in what Paul speaks of as 'the length and breadth and height and depth of the love of Christ'. (Eph 3:18-19) This vision of love, expressed in human terms by Jesus, overwhelms us with its variety and its depth, it is a vision of 'all the fullness of God' in the human face of Jesus. (2 Cor 4:6) This is the love the Spirit 'pours into our hearts' so that we get an interior knowledge of it. (Rom 5:5) It is a love we are gradually led into by the same Holy Spirit according as we are able and willing to believe in it. (Jn 16:13-15)

There are a number of well-defined kinds of love that the Spirit leads us into. We find each of these loves and the sequence in which they emerge in the course of our lives not only in the Word of God but in our personal experience as well. At the centre of these different kinds of love we are being led into is the passionate love of Jesus or what he calls the greatest expression of his love, (Jn 15:13) his love of us 'to the utmost extent'. (Jn 13:1)

A sequence of loves

Affection is a general term for the four loves that provide the foundation on which passionate love is built. As children, affection provides us with our first experience of a 'holding environment', a place where we are appreciated and accepted. Being appreciated by our parents is an important part of our experience of affection. Each stage of our growth, from our first faltering steps and the first words we speak, is noticed and delighted in by them. We also learn from our parents what it is like to be accepted when we misbehave or fall short of their expectations. A personal love we are initiated into in our home becomes more defined for us when we go to school. We do not choose our family and so it is at school when we are singled out from the crowd and chosen by our companions that we become aware of the special flavour that personal love has. When as adults we leave home and fend for ourselves we learn the meaning and value of the provident love of our parents and the meaning of the saying, 'It is care that makes and sustains us.'

Passionate love as the catalyst
When we fall in love, we get a taste of what passionate love is like and how it calls into play all the ways of loving we have already learned. The intensity of this passionate love engages our whole person in the pursuit of our beloved who becomes the centre of our world. Passionate love transforms us, takes us out of ourselves in such a way that nothing is allowed to come between us and the one we love.

> Who will separate us from the love of Christ?
> Will hardship, or distress, or persecution,
> or famine, or nakedness, or peril, or sword?
> As it is written, 'For your sake
> we are being killed all day long;
> we are accounted as sheep to be slaughtered.'
> No, in all these things we are more than conquerors
> through him who loved us.
> For I am convinced that neither death, nor life,
> nor angels, nor rulers, nor things present,
> nor things to come, nor powers, nor height, nor depth,
> nor anything else in all creation, will be able to separate us
> from the love of God in Christ Jesus our Lord. (Rom 8:35-39)

Passionate love finds fulfilment in friendship
Passionate love needs to develop other loves if it is to continue transforming us. This group of loves takes its name from the one it finds fulfilment in, the love called *friendship*. However, for friendship to emerge, passionate love must become permanent and profound. Our love becomes permanent as we learn to accept the weak and wayward side of ourselves and to affirm all the ways we 'participate in the divine nature'. (1 Pet 1:4) Our love becomes profound as we go on the journey into this 'participation' and gradually become convinced of the fact that we are loved by Jesus in exactly the same way as he is loved by his Father. (Jn 17:23) This love which shares 'everything' of the

inner life of the Trinity is what Jesus calls friendship (Jn 15:15) and at the core of this friendship is the joyful love Jesus wants us to share in, the 'complete' joy of the Trinity. (Jn 15:9-15)

> Gift better than himself God doth not know;
> Gift better than his God no man can see.
> This gift doth here the giver given bestow;
> Gift to this gift let each receiver be.
> God is my gift, himself he freely gave me;
> God's gift am I, and none but God shall have me.
> (Robert Southwell)

Jesus invites us to abide in the various kinds of love he has for us with the words, 'As the Father has loved me, so I have loved you; abide in my love'. (Jn 15:9-10) He goes on to explain that we can abide in his love by getting our whole person, 'heart, soul, mind and strength', involved in receiving his love and in responding to it. In practice, we can do this by reading a gospel story and noticing what it says to us about the way Jesus loves someone in the story. We can then let him say this love to us and after we have savoured his love and its attractiveness or beauty for some time we can tell him how we feel about this. By conversing with Jesus in this way we become more and more convinced of his love and learn to believe in it.

AN EXERCISE: Notice and record some of the different kinds of love which were aroused and became real for you as you read the sequence of loves listed above. Recall an experience of someone whom you associate with one of these loves and relive the experience by telling the story of what happened. Next, choose a gospel story in which Jesus loves in a similar way to the person in your experience and then dwell with him being like this for you now.

CHAPTER 7

The growth of interior knowledge

In the film *Lorenzo's Oil* we see a sharp contrast between two kinds of knowledge. There is the inner knowledge of the parents of Lorenzo who suffers from a disease called ALD. This means that he has only two years to live and that the lead-up to his death will be very painful. His parents refuse to accept the fact that he must die. Then there is the exterior knowledge expressed in the detached views of the doctors and scientists who do not get emotionally involved as they objectively research the case. In the end it is the interior knowledge generated by the all-encompassing love of the parents for their child that leads them to find a cure for the child's condition.

Interior and exterior knowledge
The culture we live in has a diminished sense of an inner world and the interior knowledge we find there. We are preoccupied with the outer world created by science, economics and consumerism. This fixation with the material world and with work, with information and with ideas leaves little time for reflection, for relationships and for learning the lessons that love wants to teach us. At the end of his life Charles Darwin commented thus on how 'atrophied' areas of his life had become as a result of his lack of attention to such things as music and poetry.

> My mind seems to have become a kind of machine for grinding general laws out of large collections of facts. If I had to live my life again I would have made a rule to read some poetry and to listen to some music at least once a week, for perhaps the parts of my brain now atrophied could have thus been kept active through use. The loss of these tastes is a loss of happiness.

Involving our whole person: body and soul, mind and heart
We know what interior knowledge is like when we remember the significant people and events of our story. Over the years we have accumulated a lot of this experience and when we return to it we find that the knowledge it yields is quite different from the information and ideas that make up our exterior knowledge. Significant experiences say something important to us about ourselves and also about the people involved in them and often arouse strong feelings in us. These experiences can also put us in touch with the deepest level at which we relate, the level of the convictions we have formed about what is true and worthwhile for us.

In a book called *Portraits*, Dan Berrigan describes the people who influenced his life and how the memory of them still moves him. In one of these portraits he describes the impression he retains of the way his mother looked at him when he misbehaved. He tells how at Sunday Mass she would turn from her prayer to attend to the rambunctious child at her side, gravely shake her head in disapproval and then turn back to the altar. He tells us 'there was a sweetness and suavity, even an elegance in the gesture. It impressed itself, that turn of the beautiful head from profile to full face and back. The universe was attending to me. The motion met the soft wax of the child's mind; the wax was cast in the metal we name memory; it rests there to this day.'

Awakening dormant wisdom
In our first three chapters we considered the knowledge that is available to us through the three mutually enriching circles of our personal, universal and Bible experience. However, much of this rich body of experience is dormant and if we are to reap its richness we need to arouse it, understand what it says to us and make our own of this. The knowledge that comes from this kind of reflection is the fruit of our senses, mind, heart and the intuitive power of our soul. This knowledge is not just ideas but a set of convictions that shape our lives more than any other kind of knowledge.

The disciples were discussing Lao Tzu's saying, 'Those who know do not say; those who say do not know.' When the Master entered they asked him its exact meaning. 'Which of you knows the fragrance of the rose?' When they all said they knew he asked them to put this in words. They were all silent.

The knowledge the Spirit leads us into

Interior knowledge takes on a much deeper meaning when we look at it within the context of the word of God. Central to the word is the Father's desire to reveal himself as love for each person, a love Jesus makes visible and of which the Spirit gives us an interior knowledge. We can draw on this essential source of interior knowledge when we contemplate a gospel story. Through the Spirit's enlightenment we are given glimpses of Jesus' love in the sensate details of each story and then through the Spirit's attraction we are drawn to make our own of these glimpses. In this way the Spirit 'leads us into all the truth' or into a vision of the glory of God revealed in the face of Jesus. This is the ultimate interior knowledge, for in the face of Jesus we come face to face with God our Father. 'Philip said to him, "Lord, show us the Father, and we will be satisfied." Jesus said to him, "Have I been with you all this time, Philip, and you still do not know me? Whoever has seen me has seen the Father".' (Jn 14:7-9)

John continues to develop this theme when he depicts Jesus as centring his life on making the Father known to us so that we can know the love of the Father just as Jesus does. (Jn 10:14-15, 17:26)

An interior knowledge born of Jesus' love

Coming to know the love of God our Father in this intimate way that Jesus and his Spirit make it known opens up for us a way of viewing our faith as an interior knowledge born of a growing ability to immerse our whole person in Jesus' love. This view of our faith is an enriching companion to that which sees faith as our unending quest to understand and define the eternal truths that form the foundation on which our lives as Christians rest. Paul believes that the love of God cannot be grasped but it can be known through an awareness of it that love gives. 'I pray that you may have the power to comprehend, with all the saints, what is the breadth and length and height and depth, and to know the love of Christ that surpasses knowledge, so that you may be filled with all the fullness of God.' (Eph 3:14-19) The Jerusalem Bible comments as follows on these verses: Our experience of God's love 'is more like knowing that one is loved by the other than knowing the other that one loves'. The exercise that follows aims at gaining this kind of interior knowledge of being loved rather than the kind that comes from thinking about a gospel story and its implications.

AN EXERCISE.

1 After quietening yourself, focus your attention on God's presence and on the fact that he wants to reveal this love to you.

2 Read the story of Jesus' meeting with Zacchaeus in Lk 19:1-10 and focus on what aspect of Jesus' love it reveals to you. For example, you might focus on the glimpse it gives you of Jesus' acceptance or appreciation of Zacchaeus, his concern for his welfare or his sense of Zacchaeus' dignity. Choose a word or a phrase to capture and savour the aspect of Jesus you decide to focus on.

3 Take time to let the attractiveness of this aspect of Jesus' love grow. It may help to ponder the way someone you know radiates this kind of love.

4 Put words on how, in effect, Jesus might express the aspect of his love for Zacchaeus you are focusing on. Let Jesus say these words to you a number of times so that the love they express may sink in. Stay with what Jesus says to you for as long as you can because listening to this and expressing the feelings it arouses is the deepest source of interior knowledge and the heart of prayer.

5 Finally, tell Jesus how you feel about what he says to you. For example, you may find one part of you resists what he says while another part of you welcomes it with gratitude, hope or joy.

CHAPTER 8

The glory within

The film, *Marvin's Room*, tells the story of two sisters who sought to fulfill their dreams in two very different ways. One who had married and later divorced had two teenage sons. The other was single and spent her time looking after her elderly parents, her father who was bedridden and almost incoherent and her mother who was in her dotage. The film centres on a visit the married sister pays to her parents and how she discovers that though she had married, had children and a good job, she does not feel fulfilled but is at odds with life. Her sister who spends her days looking after her parents and seems to have chosen a very difficult way of life has an aura or radiance about her.

What is glory or beauty?

In chapter 5 we saw how we are created in the image of God who is love and how this makes us capable of experiencing ourselves as loved, lovable and loving. Essential to this love is its radiance or splendour that we normally speak of as beauty though in the Bible it is called glory. For example, John speaks about the glory that radiates from Jesus because he is 'full of grace and truth' or full of kind and faithful love. 'And the Word became flesh and lived among us, and we have seen his glory, the glory as of a father's only son, full of grace and truth.' (Jn 1:14)

Even though everything God created and loves is glorious and beautiful, it pertains to human beings to be conscious of this and respond to it by acknowledging God's glory and the glory which he gives us. Psalm 8 speaks of God crowning us with glory and beauty and the prophet Ezekiel speaks of God clothing us with his own splendour. (Ezek 16:8-14) We are, like Jesus on Tabor, transfigured or transformed 'from one degree of glory to another'. (2 Cor 3:18)

Beauty is an intense attractiveness which arrests, seizes our attention and enraptures us. For example, James Joyce spoke of beauty as 'aesthetic arrest' in the sense that even though we have to struggle to capture what is true and good, beauty arrests, seizes or captures us and this effect is immediate. When we perceive beauty it enraptures us and engages our whole person, heart, soul, mind, and senses. What makes love and its beauty so compellingly attractive is that we do not just desire love and its beauty but *are a hunger* for it; we are made for glory.

What is central to revelation has become sidelined
Though beauty is central to revelation and held this position until the 13th century, it has since been sidelined by all but a few. For example, when I look up an index of any of the books by the modern Christian philosopher and theologian, Bernard Lonergan, I find a lot of references to truth and goodness but none to beauty. This loss of interest in beauty began when the universities took over from the monasteries as the centres of learning. Where the monks saw their lives in terms of the Song of Songs and sought to abide in God's love by means of prayer and *lectio divina*, the universities made the understanding of the faith their main concern. As a result, what is true and good is dealt with at length in dogmatic and moral theology whereas beauty has become peripheral.

The effect on the study of revelation was immense when the true and the good were pursued almost exclusively with the mind. It meant that the senses, heart and soul, which the Bible had fully engaged in telling the story of God's revelation as love, were marginalised. When this happened the arresting glimpse of beauty that we get in the sensate details of the story of God's self-revelation as love, was marginalised too. Without the power of beauty to enrapture us, the truth studied in dogmatic theology became too intellectual and spiritual and the good studied in moral theology became legalistic and ceased to attract. In one of his sonnets G. M. Hopkins laments this loss of the sense of the grandeur of God that permeates all things and yet he is confident that under the Spirit's guidance we can resurrect it.

And for all this, nature is never spent;
There lives the dearest freshness deep down things;
And though the last lights of the black West went
Oh, morning, at the brown brink eastward, springs –
Because the Holy Ghost over the bent
World broods with warm breast and with ah! bright wings.

Where people find beauty today

Because beauty is no longer central to revelation it is now sought mainly in art and nature and hardly at all in relationships or in the love we receive and return within these. In this context, Erich Fromm's comment in his book, *The Art of Loving*, is poignant. He writes that the greatest and yet most neglected art is that of loving. This is the art the Great Commandment wants us to make central in our life. It involves becoming skilled in relating and in being loved and loving in a way that involves our whole person, body, soul, mind and heart. (Lk 10:25)

Vain is the glory of the shy,
The beauty vain of field or grove,
Unless, while with admiring eye
We gaze, we also learn to love.
(William Wordsworth)

The ultimate beauty is found in Jesus

In the Incarnation, God, who is love itself, takes on human form and gives us 'in the face of Jesus' a vision of what is truly glorious or beautiful. 'For it is the God who said, "Let light shine out of darkness," who has shone in our hearts to give the light of the knowledge of the glory of God in the face of Jesus Christ.' (2 Cor 4:6) Jesus is the most beautiful expression of what is beautiful and he gives us a glimpse of this beauty in every gospel story. This beauty is an inseparable part of what he asks us to become aware of and believe in when he calls us to repent and believe the gospel. In human terms the ultimate expression of divine beauty is the death and resurrection of Jesus. There, he gives us the greatest revelation of his love and of its beauty in loving us to 'the utmost extent'. (Jn 13:1, 15:13)

If we look for what is supremely beautiful anywhere else than in the crucified Christ, we will look in vain. *(Karl Barth)*

The most striking piece of sculpture I have ever seen portrays the crucified Christ with Mary standing on one side of the cross and John on the other. Mary is wrapped in pain as she shares all that her son is going through. What is most striking however is the depiction of John. He is in a state of ecstasy, his face aglow and his hands raised in an expression of utter exhilaration at this ultimate manifestation of Christ's love for him. He sees in the face of Jesus that he is loved 'to the utmost extent' and in this he sees Jesus' glory and his own. (Jn 13:1)

The beauty Jesus finds in us

In seeing the glory or beauty of Jesus we also see our own glory or beauty in his eyes. We see this in the way he relates with and treats the people he meets in the gospel stories. We are challenged by one of the prefaces of the Mass to believe that the Father also sees us in this way. In it we are invited to say to our Father, 'you see and love in us what you see and love in Christ'. If we are this loved and lovable, we radiate the splendour of this love and thus share in Jesus' glory as he invites us to. (Jn 17:22)

> God has not only delivered us from sin. He has made us beautiful, lovable and attractive. (John Chrysostom)

The glimpses of Jesus' love we are given in the gospels, at Mass and during the day, challenge us to believe that we are, like John, Jesus' beloved disciple in whom he delights. The Spirit leads us into this love and into the beauty that Jesus finds in us. 'We are transfigured in ever-increasing splendour into his own image, and the transformation comes from the Lord who is the Spirit.' (Jn 16:13, 2 Cor 3:18)

AN EXERCISE: Reflect for a little while on someone you admire and then tell a story where a quality you find attractive in this person emerges. Now let this person look at you in this way and notice the sense of significance this gives you. Does the memory of this person's love reveal something attractive, radiant or beautiful about you? Try to put words on this and on how it makes you feel.

CHAPTER 9

Finding glory in each other

There is a very moving moment in the film *Calendar Girls*
when Jim who is terminally ill with cancer tells his wife of
the glory he has seen grow within her. He says to her,
'The women of Yorkshire are like the flowers of Yorkshire; every stage of their growth is more beautiful than
the last; but the last phase is always the most glorious'.

What makes these words truly striking is that, at a time when
we no longer associate beauty with the way people relate, a man
would notice the glory in his wife's life and be willing to express
it so eloquently. Yet, there is every reason why we should help
others to find their true worth, to believe in the glory that is
theirs as human beings and more so as Christians. In realising
this dignity or glory we are but accepting the extraordinary offer
of Jesus that we would share with him his own glory. (Jn 17:22)
'Christians, realise your dignity!' (St Leo the Great)

It is difficult for us to accept the glory that Jesus wants to
share with us because of the trouble it takes to find and make
our own of this pearl of great price. (Mt 13:46) It is as if we are
given an uncut diamond at the beginning of our lives and that
our life's work consists in cutting and polishing the diamond
until all its splendour is revealed.

In Search of the Priceless Jewel
There was once a man who came across a cave on his journey and being curious he entered it. There he discovered,
in the form of a priceless jewel, what was to be the inspiration of his life. However, all he could do was gaze at the
jewel as it was in the clutches of a ferocious beast. As he
gazed, his whole being was engaged and when eventually
he left he felt that all else in life from then on would be insignificant by comparison. But he got on with life, mar-

ried and reared a family and then when his life's work was done he said, 'Before I die, I must glimpse again the jewel that has been the inspiration of my life.' So he set out and made his way back to the cave where once again he found the jewel. But now the monster guarding it had grown so small that he was able to take the jewel away with him. As he made his way back home he gradually realised what it all meant. The jewel symbolised something he had discovered in himself and all his life he had been struggling with the fearsome beast or his own demons to take possession of this jewel.

If we are to help others discover and own the glory Jesus shares with them we must first learn to believe that this glory is ours. We must also remember that though we may act as a mirror in which others may see themselves, we cannot believe in this for them.

> Though we travel the world over to find the beautiful, we must carry it with us or we find it not. *(R. W. Emerson)*

Our ever-increasing splendour

There are a number of areas of glory or beauty we need to be aware of in ourselves and in others. The first of these is the glory of our body as the inseparable companion and revealer of our spirit. As Christians we believe that the body is to share in our resurrection as even now it shares in our transfiguration. (2 Cor 3:18) This view of the body as sharing our spirit's glory is resisted by distorted ways of seeing the body. For example, we may see the body as holding the spirit captive or as a source of temptation and limitation. The consumer culture we live in tends to demean the body with a view to making us feel inadequate so that we will then buy what will alleviate this inadequacy. Therefore, we need to reclaim the beauty of the body as wondrous in its own right and in the way it manifests the spirit.

> Every visible or invisible creature is a theophany or manifestation of God. *(John Scotus Erigena)*

The most ordinary kind of glory

There is a unique style of relating, a presence and aura that each of us develops in our efforts to communicate. It is a style of relating we need to notice and appreciate first of all in ourselves, for if we do not find it in ourselves we will not find it in others and more seriously still we will not find it in Jesus in the gospel stories. The art of relating or communicating is contributed to by language, gesture, demeanour and by that delicate refinement of manners we call courtesy. This art creates something so beautiful that we can say with the poet that 'The Grace of God is in Courtesy.' Yet, because it dresses in such ordinary clothes its beauty or glory can easily be missed. All this means that the best and most beautiful area of our lives can be in ordinary living.

I am sure it was from those days that I take the belief that the best of life is lived quietly, where nothing happens but our calm journey through the day, where change is imperceptible and the precious life is everything. *(John McGahern, Memoir)*

People who radiate good feeling

A second aspect of the glory we find in those around us is the aura they create by the positive or negative feelings they choose to live with. A sunny disposition is as infectious as a sad one. We are attracted by the radiance given out by people who are grateful for the past, joyful about the present and enthusiastic about the future. A very different atmosphere is created by people who complain about the past, are sad about the present and cynical about the future.

The fruit of the Spirit

The third way we find and affirm people's glory is by noticing the glimpses they give us of their unique style of loving. The people we meet each day have developed an art of loving and it is important that we notice this and ask them to believe in it. As a student of the Enneagram I have become aware of the distinct style of loving that is peculiar to each of its nine types of people and of how Grace radiates in a distinctive way from each of them. Unless we notice this Grace in ourselves and in others, people's real greatness can pass us by unnoticed and unappreciated.

This third kind of glory we find in those around us is, when it matures, what Paul calls the 'fruit of the Spirit'. This fruit appears as the Spirit brings to perfection in us a series of manifest-ations of love. These glimpses of love are often inconspicuous so that we need to develop an eye for them in ourselves and in others. Paul lists them as, 'joy, peace, patience, kindness, generosity, faithfulness, gentleness, and self-control'. (Gal 5:22)

> It is not possible for a Christian's light to be hidden. So re-splendent a light cannot be concealed.' *(John Chrysostom)*

Faith in a shared glory
A fourth way we can assist others to discover the glory of their lives is by helping them to be aware of and to believe in their own inner wisdom. When we reflect on the lives of those we admire, what is most striking or noble about them is this wisdom or the vision and the values they have lived out of, the virtues that have led them to relate and love in a way that is distinctly theirs. Therefore, anything we can do to help people to become aware of and to believe in what we admire most about them, that their lives 'are charged with the grandeur of God', is the greatest service we can do them.

> Folks want a lot of loving every minute –
> The sympathy of others and their smile;
> Till life's end, from the moment they begin it,
> Folks need a lot of loving all the while.

AN EXERCISE: Take a deeper look at a friend you admire. Notice what strikes you about the distinct style of relating he or she has. What impresses you most about this person's capacity to love? Recall an incident in which you got a glimpse of this. What intimations of this person's inner wisdom, vision and values, impress you most? Read Gal 5:22 and 1 Cor 13:4-7 and see how much of this picture of love you find in your friend. Meet this person you admire in some quiet place and talk about how you admire each other.

CHAPTER 10

The union that glory draws us into

The film, *Kramer V Kramer* is about the disintegration of a family and its subsequent reintegration. What causes the marriage to fall apart is the husband's excessive devotion to his work as this means he has little time for relating with his wife and his son. When the wife seeks a divorce and the custody of their child he has to devote his attention to the court case that ensues. As a result he loses his job and is forced into reconsidering his priorities. He realises how much his child means to him and in the course of the court case he sees things in his wife that formerly he was too busy to notice and appreciate.

What emerges from the film is how central to our dream are the basic relationships of our lives and the love that holds these relationships together. Nothing is worth sacrificing for the joy of this caring environment.

The Holding Environment
When we are infants our parents' love for us is expressed in the way they accept the limitations we impose on their lives, in their appreciation of each stage of our growth, in their ceaseless concern for our welfare and in how they convey to us that we are important for them. These different manifestations of love create what the psychologist Winnicott called 'a holding environment'. As we grow up we become more and more responsible for this environment, for expanding and maintaining it. When we leave home we have to remember and appropriate the love of our parents and build on the foundations of the caring environment they have laid.

When we fall in love we are drawn out of ourselves and into the world of the one we love. We become mutually responsible for providing an environment that will be proportionate to the love we have for each other. We will be asked to accept, appreciate and be concerned for each other in a way that makes us both feel significant and secure. If we have children we are asked to provide a holding or caring environment in which they can grow. So as we move through life we are initially receivers of love and of the environment it creates and then we are asked to share this environment and eventually to provide it for our children.

The Christian environment

For the Christian the love that makes and sustains the environment in which we live is that which the three persons of the Trinity have for each other and for us. (Jn 17:23) The Spirit gives us an intimate knowledge of the love of the Father which is expressed by Jesus in human terms. Insofar as we believe in his love we will be drawn by its radiance or glory into a union with Jesus. The intense attractiveness of this love reintegrates our relationships with ourselves, with others and with all things. 'And I, when I am lifted up from the earth, will draw all people (or all things) to myself.' (Jn 12:32) The passionate nature of Jesus' love draws us to be reconciled with or to befriend all those areas of life from which we have become estranged. John sees Jesus' death as gathering 'into one the dispersed children of God'. (Jn 11:52)

The Magnetic Field

At school we did a scientific experiment to demonstrate the magnetic field that a magnet creates. When a magnet was held under a sheet of paper with some iron filings on it they formed a very distinct pattern. Each of the filings was drawn into a relationship not only with the magnet but also with each of the other bits of iron. Even the molecules within each iron filing were influenced by the magnet. However, when the magnet was removed the filings easily reverted to their original disorder. They were no longer being held together in a definite pattern of relationships created by the magnet.

The love that creates a new order

The beauty of Jesus' love for us, especially in loving us 'to the utmost extent' can become so intensely attractive that it is capable of creating a new order. In chapters 3-12 of the book of Genesis we see how the order that God's love created is damaged by the separation and disintegration caused by sin. It is only the intensity of Jesus' love, its power to lay hold of, to seize, to capture or enrapture us that can create a magnetic field within which the right relationship of everything to everything else is re-established. 'Not that I have secured it already, nor yet reached my goal, but I am still pursuing it in the attempt to take hold of the prize for which Christ Jesus took hold of me.' (Phil 3:12)

> Yet still I hear Thee knocking, still I hear:
> 'Open to Me, look on Me eye to eye,
> That I may wring thy heart and make it whole;
> And teach thee love because I hold thee dear
> And sup with thee in gladness soul with soul,
> And sup with thee in glory by and by.
> (*Christina Rossetti*)

What we share and how we share it
The strength of the union Jesus draws us into can be gauged by what he wants to share with us, how he wants to share this and by the quality of the conversation that ensues. What Jesus wants to share with us is 'everything' that he and his Father share, their complete self-revelation and the friendship this initiates. (Jn 15:15) How we are invited to respond to this initiative of Jesus is with our whole 'heart, soul, mind and all our senses'. (Jn 15:10) To be thus receptive and responsive to God's self revelation in an ongoing way calls for regular conversation. In it we listen and respond to God's word and 'hold it fast with a noble and generous heart'. (Lk 8:15)

> Loneliness does not happen from the absence of people around us, but is experienced when the people around us do not understand what is happening inside us. (*Carl Jung*)

Images of union
Jesus compares the union our wholehearted entry into the love that he and his Father have for us to a home they come and make in us. 'Those who love me will keep my word, and my Father will love them, and we will come to them and make our home with them.' (Jn 14:23) In a home the members of the family are

drawn into a holding environment by the love of their parents and by their growing capacity to receive this love and respond to it. The bond Jesus establishes with us is even closer. He compares it to that between the vine and the branches which share the same life principle. Because we are loved by him just as he is loved by his Father we 'abide in' his love or he lives in us and we in him. '... as the Father has loved me, so I have loved you; abide in my love. (Jn 15:4, 9) For Paul we are all members of the body of Christ. 'For just as the body is one and has many members, and all the members of the body, though many, are one body, so it is with Christ. For in the one Spirit we were all baptised into one body.' (1 Cor 12:12-13)

Sharing completely the divine union

Jesus calls the union he wants to establish with us 'complete' as he draws us into his own union with the Father and the Spirit. (Jn 17:22-23) This union with Jesus is more than a union of mind and heart, it is a participation in the divine life. (2 Pet 1:4) Paul can say, 'When we cry, "Abba! Father!" it is that very Spirit bearing witness with our spirit that we are children of God, and if children, then heirs, heirs of God and joint heirs with Christ.' (Rom 8:14-17)

≀   The soul should always stand ajar, ready to welcome the ecstatic experience. *(Emily Dickinson)*

AN EXERCISE: Sketch briefly some of the main events in the story of your relationship with God the Father. Next, say how you see and feel about your relationship now and then enter into a dialogue with the Father about it. Write this down as you go along. Begin by saying how you think things are between you and then let the Father reply. Continue listening and responding honestly until you both have said all you want to say. Finish off by being quiet for a while before writing down the main insight you have been given and how you feel about this.

A culture of enjoyment

The film *It's A Wonderful Life* tells the story of a young man called George Baily who has dreams of greatness. However, when his father dies he has to sacrifice his dreams to look after their small business and those who depend on it for employment. Due to the carelessness of one of the employees the business collapses and George, feeling himself a failure, contemplates suicide. At this point his guardian angel, called Clarence, steps in. He takes George back to the main events of his life, showing him how much poorer people's lives would have been if George had not been there to help them. As a result George gets a sense of how wonderful his life has been and how true greatness is found in the ordinary.

Most of life is ordinary and it is there that most of life's joy is to be found, if we can only recognise and surrender to this reality. We often have difficulty doing this because we imagine that the last place we will find our joy is in the ordinary things we already possess.

Our distorted images of God are even a greater obstacle to finding true joy than looking for it in the wrong places. From our own experience and from that we learn from the stories people tell, we have become accustomed to images of God as serious, solemn, and perhaps weary and disappointed with us because of our poor response to his goodness. These images have deep roots in us and resist the image of God as essentially happy and as intent on our 'peace' or happiness. 'I know the plans I have in mind for you – it is Yahweh who speaks – plans for your peace, not for disaster, reserving a future full of hope for you.' (Jer 29:11)

Is love primarily concern or delight?

A major obstacle to entering this plan God has for our peace is our conviction that happiness is not an essential part of the love God is. That love is essentially delight is the contention of a doctoral dissertation of the Canadian philosopher and theologian Fred Crow. He contends that love is not primarily desire or concern, as we tend to think, but delight. He holds that even though in practice Thomas Aquinas choose to treat love as primarily concern, the prevailing belief in his writings is that love is primarily delight. If we were to take Crow's conclusion seriously, it would have a profound influence not only on our vision of God but on how intent on our happiness we judge him to be. Accepting that love is primarily delight would change radically the role we give joy in our lives and would make us more inclined to adopt a culture of enjoyment in place of our present preference for a culture of concern.

The Bible as a uniquely joyful book

Walther Eichrodt, an outstanding Old Testament scholar, believes that compared to other great literatures that of the Bible is uniquely joyous. We find a sample of this joy in the following words from Isaiah: 'You shall be a crown of beauty in the hand of the Lord, and a royal diadem in the hand of your God. You shall no more be termed Forsaken, and your land shall no more be termed Desolate; but you shall be called My Delight Is in Her, and your land Married; for the Lord delights in you, and your land shall be married. For as a young man marries a young woman, so shall your builder marry you, and as the bridegroom rejoices over the bride, so shall your God rejoice over you.' (Is 62:1-5)

Happiness as Jesus sees it

For Jesus a happiness that is both complete and constant is central to revelation. This is difficult for us to take seriously as we are inclined to see happiness as more intermittent than constant, something that comes and goes. We also associate its fullness with the next life so that the belief that we are meant to be completely and constantly happy in this life seems illusory. There is a part of us that identifies with the image of ourselves in the *Hail*

Holy Queen as 'poor banished children of Eve, weeping and wailing in this valley of tears'. Christianity has often been seen as a religion more about the cross and the sadness that surrounds it than about the glory and joy of the resurrection. From this point of view, the saying that 'the roads of the world run Heavenward every one' may seem unrealistic.

The source of the joy that Jesus offers is a vision he gives of the extent and depth of his love for us. Since this vision is of the love Jesus has for his Father and that his Father has for him the joy it leads to is a share in their own 'complete' joy. 'I have said these things to you so that my joy may be in you, and that your joy may be complete'. (Jn 15:11) However, if we are to enter this 'complete' joy, we must learn to 'abide in' their love by immersing our whole person in it, body and soul, heart and mind as the commandments would have us do. 'As the Father has loved me, so I have loved you; abide in my love. If you keep my commandments, you will abide in my love, just as I have kept my Father's commandments and abide in his love.' (Jn 15:9-10)

'The God of all consolation'

In practice, we 'abide in' Jesus' love by our faith and hope in it. Faith is an interior knowledge of this love which the Spirit pours into our hearts and constantly leads us into. Happiness always accompanies faith and is proportionate to its conviction that we are loved. This is the truth behind that wonderful saying of Victor Hugo that 'the supreme happiness in life is the conviction that we are loved'. While faith rejoices in this love we already believe in, hope gets us out on the road towards realising the full extent and depth of this love. To understand how much hope contributes to our joy it is necessary to see its connection to the poverty of spirit which is central to Jesus' teaching. This connection is based on the fact that our hope rests on God's promise to realise our dream. Therefore, if we do adopt the spirit of the beatitudes and learn to depend on God, and not just on our own effort, to find the Holy Grail we will enjoy the happiness that the beatitudes are the gateway to. 'Happy are the poor in spirit, for theirs is the kingdom of heaven'. (Mt 5:3)

A life based on faith, hope and love as well as on the poverty of spirit that hope builds on is what is called a life of consolation.

This gift of 'the God of all consolation' (2 Cor 1:3) is described as follows by St Ignatius Loyola in his *Spiritual Exercises*: 'I call consolation any increase of faith, hope and charity and any interior joy that calls and attracts to heavenly things, to the salvation of one's soul, inspiring it with peace and quiet in Christ our Lord.'

Since the persons of the Trinity are essentially joyful, and want to share their joy with us, there is every reason for cultivating a culture of enjoyment, one in which. 'all the way to heaven is heaven'. (St Catherine of Sienna) However, it will be difficult for this culture of enjoyment to take root when it has to compete with a well-established culture of concern and a consumer culture that never allows us to enjoy for long what we have. Humans seem to be the only creatures that do not believe that the main business of life is to enjoy it.

AN EXERCISE: According to Egyptian mythology we will be asked the following two questions when we seek to enter the next life: 'Did you find joy in your life?' and, 'Did you help others to find their joy?' What do you think and how do you feel as you hear these two questions? Next, outline on paper how you would answer these questions. Finally, talk to God about the answers you have given and listen to how he responds.

PART 3

Introduction

The role of the Holy Spirit in our lives is best seen in the context of the passion of the three persons of the Trinity to reveal themselves to us and that we would believe in this revelation. The Spirit brings this about by leading us bit by bit into 'all the truth' or into the love of the Father that Jesus embodies. To do this the Spirit enlightens us by highlighting some aspect of Jesus' love and by attracting us to make our own of this love. For our part, we are invited through reflection to become aware of the Spirit enlightening and attracting us and then through prayer to appropriate the love the Spirit gives us a glimpse of. The attractiveness of this love the Spirit leads us to believe in draws us into a union and joy that is proportionate to our belief.

The chapters of Part 3 begin with a history of how belief in the Spirit has developed over the centuries. We then look at the role of the Spirit within the Trinity and within their plan or dream for us. We examine the way the Spirit leads us into an interior knowledge of God's love by enlightening our minds and attracting our hearts. Next we look at how we notice the signs of the Spirit's enlightenment by reflection and the way we respond to the attractiveness of this by appropriating it in prayer. We look at reflection and prayer as the most effective ways of responding to the Spirit guiding us into belief in the good news as it is presented to us in the word of God and in the Mass. Then in the light of this vision of who God is and who we are in his eyes we see the way the Spirit enables us to discern, on the basis of the joy we experience, the best way to live consistently with this vision. We conclude Part 3 with a chapter on the union or fellowship the Spirit draws us into as she leads us into God's love and its intense attractiveness or glory. In this union and its joy we find the ultimate fulfilment of our dream.

The Holy Spirit
leads us 'into all the truth'

or *enlightens* our minds so that we glimpse
the *love* of Jesus and his Father

and *attracts* our hearts with the radiance of their love

so that we are thus drawn into the *union*
or fellowship of the Spirit
and into its *joy*

Through *reflection*
we become aware of the Spirit's enlightenment
and of the attractiveness of this

Through *prayer* we savour and assimilate this

CHAPTER 12

Nature of the Spirit as it grew in history

In the Old Covenant the Spirit was identified as the power of God at work in the world. In the exercise of this power the Spirit did not seem to be a person in the same way as the Father. Then there developed one of the earliest beliefs, formulated by the creed, which was that the Spirit spoke through the prophets. We see this in the life of Samuel who is inspired by the Spirit in a way that influences his whole being. (1 Sam 3:1-20)

As God renews his people we see the growing influence of the Spirit in the prophets. 'A new heart I will give you, and a new spirit I will put within you. And I will remove from your body the heart of stone and give you a heart of flesh.' (Ezek 36:26-28) In Jeremiah, it is revealed that God wants to make his revelation more personal and heartfelt. 'I will put my law within them, and I will write it on their hearts; and I will be their God, and they shall be my people. No longer shall they teach one another, or say to each other, "Know the Lord," for they shall all know me, from the least of them to the greatest, says the Lord.' (Jer 31:33-34) In the Acts of the Apostles Peter sees this prophecy fulfilled in the pouring out of the Holy Spirit. 'This Jesus God raised up, and of that all of us are witnesses. Being therefore exalted at the right hand of God, and having received from the Father the promise of the Holy Spirit, he has poured out this that you both see and hear.' (Acts 2:32-33)

The New Covenant sees the Spirit as a divine reality between the Father and the Son. There is a unity and a distinction between Jesus and the Spirit; Jesus is Bearer, Possessor, Proclaimer and Communicator of the Spirit but he is not the Spirit for he must go before the Spirit will come.

For John the Spirit profoundly affects our relationships, leading us into 'all the truth' or into the love of the Father that Jesus makes visible. The Spirit is poured out on Jesus at his baptism and after the Resurrection the Spirit is poured out on the church and on each person. 'God's love has been poured into our hearts through the Holy Spirit that has been given to us.' (Rom 5:5) The Spirit is a power not identical with either Father or Son but belonging to and uniting them both. This power is not named in the New Covenant but remains elusive and has no face, being represented by fire, wind, and as water.

The Fathers of the Church and the Spirit

By the 4th century there was a consensus among the Fathers about three issues: 1) The tradition that we are baptised in the name of the Father, the Son and the Holy Spirit in Mt 28:19. 2) It is clear from scripture that the Spirit is distinct from Jesus and the Father. 3) Each of the three persons has a distinctive role in the world working out a plan common to all three.

Before the Council of Sardica in 343 the Trinity was celebrated in Baptism but there was a lack of clarity about the Spirit as some identified the Spirit with Jesus as Logos. About 362 Athanasius concluded from the baptismal formula that the Spirit shared the same divinity as the Father and the Son in the unity of the same substance. In 374 Basil pronounced the doxology of 'Glory be to the Father and to the Son and to the Holy Spirit.' At Constantinople in 381 the Nicene Creed was completed, taking the form that we use today and it was confirmed in Rome in 382.

Augustine 354-430

Augustine's teaching on the Spirit is very original. The Spirit is of what is common to both Father and Son, their shared holiness and love. Being the 'community of both' the Spirit receives the names Love, Spirit and Holy. The Spirit proceeds from both Father and Son and teaches us the charity through which they love each other.

Anselm (1033-1109) does not see the Spirit as the mutual love of the Father and Son. For Anselm, the one who remembers and knows himself as the Supreme Spirit must necessarily love himself and this forms the basis for the existence of the third person. The Spirit springs from God's memory of his thought.

Richard of Saint Victor (1175) approaches the Trinity from the perspective of prayer and personal experience and says 'We must attribute to God what we regard as supreme in our scale of values and this is love or *caritas*.' This perfect charity requires a *consortium amoris* 'a loving together of a third and an enabling of that third to share in the happiness of the first two'. The Spirit is a third, equally loved or 'a common friend'. Richard follows Augustine and Anselm but instead of speaking of understanding and will, he deduces everything from love so that we have 'one love and three lovers'.

Bonaventure (1221-1274) follows Richard's theology of unselfish and communicative love, saying that mutual love is more perfect than love of self, and mutual love that communicates itself is more perfect still. The Spirit is the bond between Father and Son and is Love and Gift, the one who inspires our journey to God.

Thomas Aquinas (1225-1274) accepted that the Spirit is the bond of love between Father and Son. Very distinctive of Thomas' belief concerning the Spirit is the place he gives to the Seven Gifts of the Spirit. He linked these with the beatitudes, the virtues and the 'fruit of the Spirit' in a remarkably coherent system. These Seven Gifts centre on the theological virtues of Faith, Hope and Charity and enable us to practice them more perfectly. In this way the Gifts make us ready to grasp and follow the divine inspiration.

In the 12th and 13th centuries when people like Thomas Aquinas developed a spirituality in which the Spirit was central, there emerged the teaching of *Joachim of Fiore*. He advocated that we are living in the age when the Spirit has replaced Christ at the centre of Christian belief. Though his teaching was condemned in 1255, it continued to influence philosophy and theology down to the 19th century.

Since the Counter Reformation, the place of the Spirit has been heavily influenced by the Reformers' view of the Spirit as the one who helps us interpret scripture. The Counter Reformation saw the guidance of the Spirit happening almost exclusively within the Church. There gradually emerged from this an inflated importance given to the magisterium that seemed to replace or to diminish the role of the Spirit. As a result, the Spirit has been allowed to play only a minor role in the lives of Christians and was left out of the highly esteemed picture of the faith painted by Karl Adam in 1924.

Vatican II sought to remedy this by adopting a Trinitarian view of creation and grace. It spoke of Christians as the people of God, the Body of Christ and the temple of the Holy Spirit. The fact that the Spirit makes a new creation of the Christian was stated but not developed. Yves Congar closes the first volume of his book, *I Believe in the Holy Spirit*, with the words of Paul VI: 'The Christology and especially the ecclesiology of the Second Vatican Council should be followed by a new cult of the Holy Spirit, as an indispensable complement of the conciliar teaching.' John Paul II added his voice to this movement when he said: 'The ecclesiology of the Council must be succeeded by a new study of and a devotion to the Holy Spirit as the indispensable complement of the teaching of the Council.'

To get some idea of what this 'new cult' 'study' and 'devotion' might look like I will rely on the way the whole tradition about the Holy Spirit is presented in Yves Congar's *I Believe in the Holy Spirit* and in von Balthasar's *The Spirit of Truth*. I will focus on the two themes I outlined in the introduction to this book: the love of God that has been poured into our hearts by the Holy Spirit (Rom 5:5) and how the Holy Spirit leads us into this love. (Jn 16: 13-15)

> Through the Holy Spirit we are re-established in paradise, we have an approach to the Kingdom of Heaven, a return to our status as adopted children, the courage to call God our Father, communion with the grace of Christ, our name as children of light, participation in eternal glory and to put it simply, the entire fullness of blessing in this age and the age to come. *(St Basil 329-379)*

The role of the Spirit within the Trinity

One of the great masterpieces of Russian art is the icon painted around 1425 by the monk Andrea Rublev. It is based on the story in Genesis of the three angels who visited Abraham. (Gen 18:1-18) In the East this scene has always been interpreted as the mystery of the three persons in one God. While previous painters represented the complete scene (the three angels, Abraham, Sara and the calf) the 15th century Russian monk has given us a highly symbolic representation.

In the centre, instead of the calf, appears the Eucharistic cup, and the three angels are united in heavenly communion, one might say, on the plan of Redemption. It has been stated that 'nowhere does there exist anything similar with regard to strength of theological synthesis, the richness of symbolism, and artistic beauty'. The colours themselves have a particular luminosity and the whole picture gives an impression of profound peace in the circular movement in which the scene is set. It is generally accepted that the angel on the right represents the Holy Spirit, the angel in the centre represents the Son with the Father represented by the angel on the left. The aim of the artist, however, is not to lead us to one or other of the persons of the Trinity but to lead us to the contemplation of the essence of the mystery of the Triune God.

In the rich tradition that has built up about the relationship of these three persons, the Holy Spirit emerges as the one who clarifies and attracts us to the self-revelation of the Father and the Son. In their passion to communicate themselves the Son reveals the Father just as the Spirit does the Son. In this revelation the Son makes the Father visible while the Spirit gives us an interior knowledge of Jesus. (Jn 16:13-15)

Balthasar, in his book *The Spirit of Truth,* expressed the relationship of the three persons in the following way: 'From all eternity God is Father by eternally giving his all in a primal act of love. The Son receives this as lover, returning love in the reciprocal interplay of wonder and worship, gratitude and entreaty. The excess of this reciprocal love produces a third, just as the child is the proof and the fruit of the reciprocal love of the parents.'

And God and God and God are love merely
Until they find foolish us
To take love's overflow.
(Padraig J Daly)

The Spirit's relationship to the Father and to Jesus
Paul expresses the Spirit's relationship to the Father and Jesus in this way: 'For all who are led by the Spirit of God are sons of God … When we cry, "Abba! Father!" it is the Spirit himself bearing witness with our spirit that we are children of God, and if children, then heirs, heirs of God and fellow heirs with Christ.' (Rom 8:14-17)

With all the complexity and mysteriousness of the Trinity for the human mind, it is hard to believe what Frank Sheed says of his experience of the people who came to listen to and argue with him in London's Hyde Park.

I discovered on the street corner what no one would have guessed, and now that we have discovered it, no one will believe. Namely, that the subject of all in the Catholic Life Teaching Programme which fascinates street corner crowds is the Blessed Trinity. You can hold a crowd on the Blessed Trinity, when you can't hold them with anything else. They do not want you to go away. They will ask you to come back. The Blessed Trinity fascinates street corner crowds.

The role of the Spirit in Jesus' life
Before his baptism Jesus is not seen as one guided by the Spirit so his baptism opens up a new chapter in his life. He is now the one on whom the Spirit rests and he will thereafter act through the Spirit. 'John bore witness, "I saw the Spirit descend as a dove

from heaven, and it remained on him. I myself did not know him; but he who sent me to baptize with water said to me, He on whom you see the Spirit descend and remain, this is he who baptizes with the Holy Spirit".' (Jn 1:32) The Spirit remains with Jesus throughout his life influencing all he says and does. 'The Spirit of the Lord is upon me, because he has anointed me to preach good news to the poor. He has sent me to proclaim release to the captives and recovering of sight to the blind, to set at liberty those who are oppressed.' (Lk 4:18)

In the second half of the 4th century St Basil expressed his belief that the Spirit now works with Jesus to 're-establish us in paradise'.

> Through the Holy Spirit we are re-established in paradise, we have an approach to the Kingdom of Heaven, a return to our status as adopted children, the courage to call God our Father, communion with the grace of Christ, our name as children of light, participation in eternal glory and to put it simply, the entire fullness of blessing in this age and the age to come. We contemplate as in a mirror, as though already present, the grace of the good things stored up for us in promises, the enjoyment of which we receive through faith. If such is the pledge, how great will the perfection be? If the first fruits are so grand, what will be the fullness of all?

After his baptism the life of Jesus and that of the Spirit intertwine and are inseparable. Their roles are interdependent, complementary and complex. To describe their relationship the early Christian writers used the image of the Spirit and Jesus being the two hands of the Father; together they moulded Christians in the image of Jesus. 'In him you also, when you had heard the word of truth, the gospel of your salvation, and had believed in him, were marked with the seal of the promised Holy Spirit'. (Eph 1:13)

The Spirit who formed Jesus in Mary now forms each Christian and the church in the image of Jesus. Just as at the baptism of Jesus the Spirit remained with him and became a powerful influence on his life, so at our baptism the Spirit becomes a powerful transforming influence on us. Our lives are transformed into that of Jesus so that his relationship with the Father becomes ours and we say in him, 'Abba! Father!' 'For all who are led by the Spirit of God are children of God … When we cry, "Abba! Father!' it is that very Spirit bearing witness with our spirit that we are children of God, and if children, then heirs, heirs of God and joint heirs with Christ.' (Rom 8:14-17) For the rest of our lives, as Jesus promised, the Spirit guides us into 'all the truth' or into this loving relationship with his Father that Jesus wants to share with us. (Jn 16:13-15)

> Batter My heart, three person'd God; for, you
> As yet but knock, breathe, shine, and seeke to mend;
> That I may rise, and stand, o'erthrow mee, and bend
> Your force, to breake, blowe, burn and make me new.
> I, like an usurpt towne, to another due,
> Labour to admit you, but Oh, to no end,
> Reason your viceroy in mee, mee should defend,
> But is captiv'd, and proves weake or untrue.
> Yet dearely I love you, and would be loved faine,
> But am betroth'd unto your enemie:
> Divorce mee, untie, or breake that knot againe,
> Take mee to you, imprison mee, for I
> Except you enthrall mee, never shall be free,
> Nor ever chast, except you ravish mee.
> *(John Donne)*

AN EXERCISE: Remember and note down a few key moments in the development of your relationship with the Holy Spirit. Describe how you see and feel about the Spirit now and choose a word or phrase that captures this. Next quieten yourself by saying this word or phrase repeatedly and when you are quiet and focused let the Spirit join you. Tell the Spirit how you see and feel about her presence in your life just now. Then listen to how the Spirit replies to this and continue this conversation as long as you have something to say to each other. After your conversation, you might find it helpful to write down some of the key points that emerged from it.

The Spirit leads us into 'all the truth'

The Immortal Diamond

The uncut diamond looks much like any other stone so that its lustre is unimaginable before it is cut. It is only to the discerning eye that its splendour can be seen beneath the ordinary exterior. To realise this splendour the craftsman, with an eye for what it might be, must work with a knowing and steady hand to uncover the riches of the diamond. To cut the diamond is an arduous task for it is the hardest of stones and does not readily reveal its glory. However, when it is cut this glory has many facets, each reflecting the light in a different way, each facet rivalling the others for splendour.

It takes a lifetime to realise the supreme splendour of the reality that 'God's love has been poured into our hearts through the Holy Spirit that has been given to us'. (Rom 5:5) At the beginning of our lives this gift of the Spirit is like the uncut diamond in that the range and depth of its love is hidden. It is only when we are willing to undertake the lifelong task of painstakingly realising that, because 'God's love has been poured into our hearts', we now 'participate in the divine nature'. (2 Pet 1:4) We now live our life within the Trinity. We receive the gift of the Spirit, who personifies or epitomises this love-life of the Father and Jesus, that we might 'understand' this gift and savour its splendour. 'Now we have received not the spirit of the world, but the Spirit which is from God, that we might understand the gifts bestowed on us by God.' (1 Cor 2:12) This understanding is not just an intellectual one but comes through listening to the 'still small voice of calm' with which the Spirit inspires us as she did Elijah. (1 Kgs 19:12)

Breathe through the beats of our desire
The coolness of thy balm;
Let sense be dumb, let flesh retire;
Speak through the earthquake, wind and fire,
O still, small voice of calm.
(John Whittier)

The love 'poured into our hearts by the Holy Spirit' is what John calls 'the truth' which is the love of God, whose glory or beauty we see in the face of Jesus in each gospel story. (2 Cor 4:6) Throughout our lives the Spirit leads us into this love and its diamond-like splendour. 'When the Spirit of truth comes, he will guide you into all the truth; ... He will glorify me, because he will take what is mine and declare it to you.' (Jn 16:13-15)

An interior knowledge of love
The fact that the Spirit's love is poured 'into our hearts' is deeply significant for it means we can now attain an interior knowledge of this love. This is a knowledge that appeals to our whole person, body, heart and soul as well as our mind. As a result, we can know from personal experience 'what is the breadth and length and height and depth, and know the love of Christ that surpasses knowledge'. (Eph 3:16-19) Commenting on this knowledge 'that surpasses knowledge' the Jerusalem Bible says it is 'a mystical awareness had through love. This awareness is something deeper than scientific knowledge, cf 1 Cor 13, and is more like knowing that one is loved by the other than knowing the other that one loves, cf Gal 4:9; even awareness of this sort however can never "grasp" this kind of love.'

For he who understands that sight
Remains for aye, though knowing naught,
Transcending knowledge with his thought.
(John of the Cross)

In his book on the Spirit, Balthasar says the following about the interior knowledge that the Spirit wishes to lead us into: 'Jesus is the supreme gift of the Father to the world and a sign of absolute love, and the work of the Spirit is treated by the middle ages as one of understanding of what has been given us in the

Son. 1 Cor 2:12 The whole work of 'guiding' us into the divine nature, including everything that, in the school of Bernard, is described as *saperem sentire, praegustare* as 'tasting and knowing things from within' is unambiguously in the service of guiding into all the truth.'

An interior knowledge of life within the Trinity

We can know something of the extent and depth of God's love because we are made in God's image. (Gen 2:27) The capacity for a God-like love which this gives us lays the foundation for the new life Jesus wishes to share with us through our baptism. This life is a participation in Jesus' own relationship with his Father that the Spirit brings to be. 'For you did not receive a spirit of slavery to fall back into fear, but you have received a spirit of adoption. When we cry, "Abba! Father!" it is that very Spirit bearing witness with our spirit that we are children of God, and if children, then heirs, heirs of God and joint heirs with Christ (Rom 8:15-17)

To get a sense of and a taste for the family circle that the Spirit's love and its splendour draws us into, we need to reflect on it in the light of the warm environment our friends and family draw us into.

> The more mature human being seems to keep within his memories, to refer to in difficult times, the images of those people who have believed in him. *(Rollo May, Love and Will)*

Though it is for the most part dormant, we carry a similar memory of being loved by the Trinity because the Spirit seeks to bring to our mind all that Jesus has said to us about this relationship. 'But the Advocate, the Holy Spirit, whom the Father will send in my name, will teach you everything, and remind you of all that I have said to you.' (Jn 14:26)

What sharing in this love leads to

We have seen how the Spirit, in leading us 'into all the truth' or into an interior knowledge of Jesus' love and its glory, draws us into the family circle of the Trinity. 'God has made us welcome in the everlasting love he bears towards the Beloved'. (Eph 1:6-7)

In John chapter 17 we see how Jesus envisages this dream the Spirit has for us being fulfilled. It is a dream of love whose glory draws us into a union and a joy that is 'complete'. 'The glory that you have given me I have given them, so that they may be one, as we are one, I in them and you in me, that they may become completely one, so that the world may know that you have sent me and have loved them even as you have loved me … and I speak these things in the world so that they may have my joy made complete in themselves.' (Jn 17:22-23, 13)

> Although our view of the most sublime things is limited and weak, it is a great pleasure to catch even a glimpse of them. *(Thomas Aquinas)*

AN EXERCISE: Be in a quiet place where you like to be with a friend and let the atmosphere of the place grow on you. Recall an incident in which you became conscious of a growth in the way you loved or related. In the light of this chapter spend time identifying how the Spirit was at work in the incident you have recalled. In anticipation of meeting the Spirit decide what, in the light of your present experience, you would like to talk about. When you meet, enter a conversation in which both of you listen and respond honestly to each other. Be prepared to let the conversation go where it will. When the conversation ends, remain on in your quiet place and write down what you want to remember of your conversation.

CHAPTER 15

How the Spirit leads us 'into all the truth'

There may come a time when we don't hear the birds
Brother Boniface, an old monk, recalled how as a very
young lad he had discovered the stars but how in the
struggle to make a living he had lost sight of them. He
learned that you had to move beyond making a living if
you were to dream, to be enraptured by simple things, for
otherwise in keeping your mind on what you were doing
you forgot the sky above. He recalled that his father, to
prevent him idling, had sent him to deliver messages
from their shop to the monastery and though it was not
very exciting it gave him a chance to dream. One day, as
he cycled home he became conscious that no matter what
you did ' you had to keep your eyes upon what you were
doing, and soon you forgot that there was a sky overhead
and earth underfoot, and that flowers blew and even that
birds sang.' *(Mary Lavin , Brother Boniface)*

In a world where there are so many urgent things demanding our attention it is hard to make time for what is important, to
make time for the dream the Spirit dreams in us. In this chapter
we will look at the way the Spirit invites us to make room for the
most important thing of all, the love she pours into our hearts.
(Rom 5:5) This is what Jesus means when he speaks about the
Spirit as the one who will guide us into 'all the truth' or into the
love of the Father that Jesus makes visible and tangible, engaging and even enrapturing. 'When the Spirit of truth comes, he
will guide you into all the truth.' (Jn 16:13-15)

Jesus speaks of the Spirit as a teacher who guides us on our
journey towards realising all the potential that is ours since we
are made in God's image and remade in that of Jesus. '... the
Holy Spirit will teach you everything and remind you of all I

have said to you.' (Jn 14:26) Paul also describes the Spirit as our guide when he appeals to us to 'be guided by the Spirit'. (Gal 5:25) Like all human teaching and learning, that of the Spirit is gradual or 'by slow degrees and more and more'.

> We have no wings, we cannot soar,
> But we have feet to scale and climb,
> By slow degrees and more and more,
> The cloudy summit of our time.
> *(Longfellow)*

The Spirit, in her respect for our freedom, teaches us only what we are able and willing to learn (2 Cor 3:17) and does this by gently enlightening our minds and attracting our hearts. It is important that we understand the nature of this enlightenment and attraction if we are to be open to it.

How the Spirit enlightens us

We may think of the word enlightenment in terms of the understanding the Spirit gives us of the eternal truths of our faith. Here, however, we are interpreting enlightenment in the more experiential way that Henri de Lubac did when he said that it is not an idea but the way someone looks at you. We are familiar with this kind of enlightenment from the way people look at, relate with or treat us. In this context we can understand the way the Spirit enlightens us by giving us a glimpse of Jesus' love from the way he relates with us in a gospel story.

The way the Spirit attracts us

When the Spirit enlightens us or gives us a glimpse of love, there is an inbuilt attractiveness about it as there is about all love. The more we get to know this love interiorly the more attractive it can become for us. The love that the Spirit pours into our hearts and leads us into has a beauty beyond all else as it is the glory of God shining out of the face of Jesus. (2 Cor 4:6) In every gospel story the Spirit offers us a glimpse not only of Jesus' glory but of our own too. For we become like Moses, who after speaking with God was 'alight with heavenly splendour'. (2 Cor 3:7) But it is not just from contemplating Jesus in a gospel story that we see this glory for it is on offer in all human love. Even though this love is limited, the glimpses we get of it and of its glory can put us in touch with the love of the Spirit and make this love and its beauty more real and engaging.

'Where the Holy Ghost in flame has signed'

The Spirit enlightens and attracts us within three important areas of our experience that are all the more important for being mutually enriching. Within our *personal experience* the Spirit teaches us much about love through the people in our own story and within our more *universal experience* we are often inspired by the stories other people tell us. But the Spirit speaks most clearly and movingly through *God's Word* as the story of God's self-revelation. Though we tend to separate these three areas within which the Spirit seeks to influence us, her voice is most enlightening and engaging when all three are combined. When we separate them we tend to undervalue the profound influence of the Spirit in the most ordinary life. 'Let us hang upon the lips of all the faithful for the Spirit of God is upon every one of them.' *(Paulinus of Nola)*

Reflection and prayer

The most effective way we can listen and respond to the enlightenment and attraction of the Spirit is through reflection and prayer. Through reflection we pay attention to the gentle way that love emerges in the glimpses we are given of it in our own story, in the stories others tell and in the gospel stories. We also notice that this enlightenment is from the Holy Spirit for this is what makes it really important. If we can put words on what we have noticed we can clarify the glimpses of love the Spirit inspires and in time make our own of these.

> With stammering lips and insufficient sounds
> I strive and struggle to deliver right
> the music of my nature.
> *(Elizabeth B. Browning)*

Through prayer we savour and assimilate the glimpses of love and of its attractiveness we have noticed and named through reflection. By listening and responding to the Spirit's enlightenment and attraction in prayer we enter the basic dia-

logue the Spirit draws us into and say with Jesus, 'Abba! Father!'
'God has sent the Spirit of his Son into our hearts, crying Abba!
Father!' (Gal 4:6) In this prayer the Spirit inspires we listen to
who we essentially are and express our wholehearted response
to this awesome reality of being in Christ before the Father.
(Rom 8:14-17) What we are invited to believe in here is so awe-
inspiring that it is bound to be resisted even though we are so
profoundly in need of this relationship which we are made for.

Why dost thou shade thy lovely face? O, why
Does that eclipsing hand so long deny
The sunshine of thy soul-embracing eye?

Without that Light, what light remains in me?
Thou art my Life, my Way, my Light; in thee
I live, I move, and by thy beams I see.

Thou art the pilgrim's path, the blind man's Eye,
The dead man's Life; on thee my hopes rely.
If thou remove, I err, I grope, I die.
(Francis Quarles)

AN EXERCISE: Recall an experience in which, at the time or af-
terwards, you were conscious of the Spirit's guidance and notice
how you responded to this. On reflection, what image of the
Spirit emerges from this experience? What qualities of the Spirit
as your guide are you most conscious of? Meet the Holy Spirit in
some quiet space and talk about the place you have given her
and what place you would now like to give her in your life.

CHAPTER 16

Reflection

The true story told in the film *Awakenings*, is set in a psychiatric hospital in New York. The patients there have an illness which leaves them in a sleep-like state. A doctor, whose whole life seems to be lived in his head, comes to the hospital. Through his research he finds a way of awakening the patients and for a short time they live active and full lives. He cannot, however, keep them like this, so they revert to their sleep-like state.

At the end of the film the doctor realises that his spirit has undergone a similar awakening. He sees, through his care for the patients and the effects of this care on them, that a whole field of experience has been awakened in him. He recognises that he must find a way to nourish his spirit and to awaken whole areas of his life that have been dormant. The film ends with the following commentary by the doctor on what has happened. 'The Summer was extraordinary, a season of rebirth and innocence; a miracle for fifteen patients and their caretakers. But now we have to adjust to the realities of miracles. We can hide behind Science and say it was the drug that failed or that the illness itself had returned or that the patients were unable to cope with losing decades of their lives. The reality is that we do not know what went wrong or what went right. What we do know is that as the chemical window closed another awakening took place, that the human spirit is more powerful than any drug and that this needs to be nourished with work, play, friendship and family. These are the things that matter. This is what we have forgotten; the simplest things.'

Reflection is the main way we awaken to what is going on below the surface of our lives. Through it we develop our capacity to notice and understand what is significant in our experience. However, the habit of reflection comes at a price for it demands that we make the space or the time, energy and resourcefulness reflection calls for.

> You must have a room or a certain hour of the day when you do not know what was in the morning paper ... a place where you can simply experience and bring forth what you are and what you might be ... *(Joseph Campbell)*

What we make space in our life to reflect on
The main thing we make space for when we reflect is God's self-revelation as love. This as we have seen comes to us through the enlightenment and attraction of the Spirit. There is, however, an-other voice at work besides that of the Spirit which reminds us of the reality that in many situations we do not feel accepted or ap-preciated. Our tendency to believe this voice rather than that of the Spirit makes the doughnut principle, that we keep our eye on the doughnut and not on the hole, central to reflection.

Keeping our eye on the doughnut
Our tendency to keep our eye on the hole in the doughnut or on the 10% of life that is deficient means that it easily becomes the 90% of what we see. This illusion or distorted vision of reality in which our significance is questioned, leads to a variety of nega-tive feelings such as frustration, guilt, sadness, hopelessness, fear and anxiety. There are three levels at which we experience this illusion about ourselves. At first we will notice how a nega-tive feeling, such as anger, can dominate our day and lead us to see our day in a negative light. We move down to a deeper level of illusion when a negative feeling such as anger becomes habit-ual and colours the way we see ourselves. At the deepest level this illusion of a poor self-image hinders or blocks our accept-ance of the affirmation of others and our belief in the love Jesus has for us. This loss of faith in ourselves and the resulting loss of joy is often accompanied by a loss of hope that we experience as a lowering of enthusiasm.

Because faith in Jesus' love is the main source of joy in the New Covenant and hope is the main source of enthusiasm, any diminishment of our faith and hope is accompanied by a loss of our joy and enthusiasm. Since joy and enthusiasm are such basic needs we tend to seek them elsewhere if we do not find them in Jesus; we tend to seek them in places where the joy and enthusiasm we get is often superficial, fragile and temporary.

Dealing with the daily erosion of our faith and hope
It is this loss of joy and enthusiasm that Jesus noticed when he met his two disciples on the road to Emmaus. When he joined them, their faith and hope were at a low ebb and they were sad and in despair. However, after being with Jesus their joy and enthusiasm were restored. We may ask ourselves how Jesus did this and how he might do the same for us. It is worth noticing that first of all he invites us to notice what is troubling us so that we can articulate it or 'whisper it to ourselves' and to someone like him who is strong enough to hear what troubles us. To name the demon is to slay him.

> If you have a fearful thought, do not share it with someone who is weak, whisper it to yourself and ride on singing. *(Alfred)*

Naming our experience, as the novelist Rebecca West says, helps us to clarify it or to bring it into focus. 'I can remember things only if I have a pencil and I write with it and I can play with it. I think your hand concentrates for you. I don't know why it should be so.'

After Jesus has listened to the part of our story we have told him about, he will want to accept us where we are. (Lk 19:1-10) He will also identify with us in our weaknesses and temptations because being human he is familiar with all of them. (Heb 4:15) He will want to put our weakness and sinfulness in perspective by highlighting all that is positive in the situation he finds us in. (Lk 7:36-50) Finally, he will delight in our struggle with weakness for it is often in this struggle that we are most heroic: he will want to assure us that he loves us most where we love ourselves least. (Lk 15:1-7)

The Emmaus road experience restores our perspective and allows us to see our limitations and sinfulness against the background of the enduring love of Jesus. We see this in the way he unfolds what the Word of God and the Eucharist have to say to us about his enduring, passionate and all-encompassing love. This love frees us from being dominated by our deficiencies and frees us to hear what is positive about ourselves as we learn to see ourselves and others in Jesus' eyes. Believing in his love and the glory or sense of deep significance it gives us is a lifetime's work but every step we take towards faith and hope in this love is accompanied by an increase of joy and enthusiasm.

As our belief in Jesus' love grows, so does our ability to see all in its radiant light. Everyone and everything, no matter how apparently insignificant, become a sign of this love. As such everything puts us in touch with the love of Jesus at the centre of our lives. Thus, everything becomes a source of faith and its joy, of hope and its enthusiasm, of gratitude and praise.

> A Heart to praise thee
> Thou hast given so much to me
> Give me one thing more – a grateful heart:
> Not thankful when it pleaseth me,
> As if thy blessings had spare days,
> But such a heart whose Pulse may be
> Thy Praise.
> (George Herbert)

AN EXERCISE: Recall to mind some issue that has been bothering you in recent times. Notice how you feel as you recall it. Next, sit with Jesus and be quiet in his presence. Then let him ask you how you are and in response tell him about what has happened and how it makes you feel. Ask him how he feels about you and then listen to his acceptance of you as you are. Listen also to his appreciation of all the good he finds in you. You may find it helpful to look at the way Jesus accepts and appreciates the woman in Simon's house in Lk 7:36-50.

Prayer as a time to remember

The film *The Horse Whisperer* provides us with a symbol of
the struggle required if we are to establish and maintain
intimate relationships with others. The film tells the story
of Tom and of how he helps a horse involved in a horrific
accident to overcome the effects of this trauma. Tom also
has to cope with the after-effects on the young girl who
was riding the horse at the time of the accident. She is
dealing with the shock of the accident, with having her
leg amputated and with what has happened to her horse.
Added to these problems are those of the girl's parents.
The way Tom wrestles with these problems is a symbol of
how each of us has to struggle to establish and maintain
our relationships. We come to these with our own unique
traumas that events from the past may have generated.
Like the horse, when we are wounded, we tend to keep
others at a distance for fear that they might touch or open
up again these wounds from our past.

In depicting Tom's efforts to establish a relationship
with the horse there is a marvellously symbolic scene in
the film when the horse manages to escape into a large
field. Rather than trying to recapture the horse, Tom sits
for most of the day in the middle of the field. Towards
evening the horse begins to draw near and eventually
makes contact with Tom. As well as listening, being sensitive and receptive to where the horse is, Tom also responds by challenging the horse to enter into relationship
with him.

It may seem unusual to portray what is going on in prayer in
terms of the story told in *The Horse Whisperer* but this may be because we do not think of prayer as the communication essential
to relationship. However, if we assume, as this chapter does,

that prayer is essentially conversation and that our relationships will be as good as this ability to communicate, then prayer is basic to life, to the way life educates us.

> The primary task of the schoolteacher is to teach children, in a secular context, the technique of prayer. *(W. H. Auden)*

Prayer as a conversation the Spirit engages us in
Our most basic relationship, and that on which all others depend, is with God and the conversation through which we maintain this relationship is the kind of prayer we will look at in this chapter. It is initiated by the Spirit leading us into 'all the truth' or into the love of God that Jesus puts in flesh and blood terms. (Jn 16:13) Therefore, the first thing the Spirit asks us to do is to listen to this revelation and then that we would respond to what we have listened to as honestly as we can. Of the two, listening is more important and the more difficult but responding honestly to what we have listened to is vital to the growth of our relationship with God.

> When feelings are very strong, affective prayer is possible, only if the person can put them before the Lord and let him accept them. Otherwise, the unnoticed negative feelings will stand like a ridge between him and the Holy One. *(Barry and Connolly, The Practice of Spiritual Direction)*

Prayer as central to the call of the gospel
As we have seen, it is the role of reflection to notice and to name the glimpses of love and its glory the Spirit gives us, whereas it is the role of prayer to savour and assimilate these glimpses by listening and responding to them. When we assimilate these glimpses they become the convictions about Jesus' love that faith consists in. In the gospels this faith is inseparable from repentance, and even though we may associate repentance with being sorry for the wrongs we have done, it is essentially about changing the way we see and feel about God, ourselves and others. If we are to accept the way Jesus sees and feels about us, we have to let go of ways of seeing him and seeing ourselves that are at variance with this. Otherwise we will allow distorted ways of seeing him and ourselves to block the love he asks us to believe in. Because our convictions about what is true and what

is worthwhile have become so ingrained, changing them is extremely difficult. It is as if our vision and values form a tough shell that we are comfortable within and therefore reluctant to change.

> There is a certain kind of crab that lives in a shell but not the one shell for life. As it grows it must discard the old shell that it has outgrown or it will die. Changing shells is not easy for the old one has to be split open and the crab becomes very vulnerable until a new one has grown. When its shell becomes too thick, too tough to crack open, the crab cannot grow any more. That is when it dies.

The difficult task that prayer undertakes
Our shells are not as visible as those of the crab but they are as real. We have difficulty repenting or freeing ourselves from limited or distorted ways of seeing things and the negative feelings that accompany these just as we have difficulty replacing these with the good news and the consolation it brings with it. Jesus highlights this difficulty in his parable about the seven evil spirits. 'When the unclean spirit has gone out of a person, it wanders through waterless regions looking for a resting place, but not finding any, it says, "I will return to my house from which I came." When it comes, it finds it swept and put in order. Then it goes and brings seven other spirits more evil than itself, and they enter and live there; and the last state of that person is worse than the first.' (Lk 11:24-26)

Lectio Divina
Over the centuries, prayer, understood as a conversation, has established itself as the most effective way of answering the essential call of the gospels to repent and believe the good news. (Mk 1:14-15) We will conclude this chapter with an outline of a way of praying called *Lectio Divina* that the Spirit has led people to adopt in order to bring about this change.

This way of praying was initially developed by the Benedictines and became basic to the prayer of monastic life. It is built around the image of the ladder in Jacob's dream, a ladder stretching between heaven and earth with the angels of God descended and ascended it. (Gen 28:10-17) This is a symbol of

God's descent in self-revelation and our listening as well as of
our ascent to God in our worship and self-surrender. George
Herbert, in a poem called *Prayer*, portrays the richness of this
exchange between heaven and earth:

> Prayer the Church's banquet, Angels age,
> God's breath in man returning to his birth,
> The soul in paraphrase, heart in pilgrimage,
> The Christian plummet sounding heav'n and earth:
> ... Heaven in ordinary, man well dressed,
> The milky way, the bird of Paradise:
> Church bells beyond the stars heard, the soul's blood,
> The land of spices, something understood.

THE EXERCISE

1 Quieten yourself in some way like listening to sounds. Then
focus your attention on God with the help of a word or phrase
that engages you. For instance, you might let God say to you a
number of times, 'I am with you.'

2 Read a piece of God's word, such as Deut 1:29-33, a few times
to see what aspect of God's love it reveals to you. Take time to
put words on and to admire the glimpse it gives you, for example,
of God's willingness to stay with you.

3 Put words on how, in effect, God might express this love to
you. He might say to you something like, 'I am always with you
no matter where you go or what you do.'

4 Let God say these words to you a number of times to let the
love they express sink in. Stay with what God says to you as
long as you can.

5 Tell God how you feel about what he says to you. You may
find that one part of you resists what God says to you while
another part welcomes it with feelings such as gratitude, hope
or joy.

CHAPTER 18

Contemplating Jesus in the Gospels

Cyrano de Bergerac was a man with an unusually large nose and this became the dominant feature of the way he saw himself. He was a very noble person but because of his slight disfigurement he could not accept the love of Roxanne even though he craved for it. At the end of the story, when Roxanne has developed a profound love for Cyrano, one feels like saying to him, 'Would you forget about your nose and accept her love, and all the life and happiness that it will bring you.' However, Cyrano cannot believe in her love for him and so he dies, a sad and lonely man.

It is our basic tragedy that we believe other voices rather than that of Jesus. As a result we succumb, like Cyrano did, to the illusion of our insignificance and thus we take the way to 'destruction'. If we are to take the narrow and more difficult road to 'life', we must learn to believe in the way Jesus sees and feels about us. (Mt 7:13-14)

Who do you say I am?
The question, 'Who do you say I am?' that Jesus asked his disciples, after they had time to get to know him, is one he asks us in every gospel story. He asks this question because his one objective in every gospel story is to make known in his human person the full extent and depth of his Father's love for us. He knows that in believing in this love we will attain the life and happiness he has come to give us in abundance. (Jn 10:10, 15:11) Even though we have tended to make the meaning of the gospel stories and their moral implications the focus of our attention, Jesus' primary concern in each story is to give us an intimate knowledge of his love. Thus the object of our prayer is to be loved and

to love rather than to think, for 'by love he can be caught and held, but by thinking never'. *(The Cloud of Unknowing)*

An intimate knowledge of Jesus

When those who had never met Jesus asked his disciples who Jesus was they decided to put together a collection of stories that would portray Jesus as they had come to know him. They said in effect to those who wanted to meet Jesus, 'Read these stories and, guided by the Spirit, you will come to know Jesus as we have.' Therefore, in telling these stories Matthew, Mark, Luke and John are inviting us to meet and come to know Jesus in the way they themselves were invited to meet and come to know him. 'When Jesus turned and saw them following, he said to them, "What are you looking for?" They said to him, "Rabbi", "where are you staying?" He said to them, "Come and see." They came and saw where he was staying, and they remained with him that day. It was about four o'clock in the afternoon.' (Jn 1:38-39) If we accept Jesus' invitation, 'Come and see', we will come to know the love he essentially is. We also come to know his glory, which is the radiance, splendour or beauty of his love. '... we have seen his glory, the glory as of the Father's only Son, full of grace and truth.' (Jn 1:14)

> When it is a question of our justification we have to put away all thinking about the Law and our works, to embrace the mercy of God alone, and to turn our eyes away from ourselves and upon Jesus Christ alone. *(John Calvin)*

As we read the gospels, the Spirit enlightens and attracts us or gives us an intimate knowledge of Jesus' kind and faithful love, his 'grace and truth' and of its glory. The Spirit fosters this interior knowledge by encouraging us to become engaged in two important areas of our experience. The first is our experience of those who have given us an impression of what love and its glory is like. The second is that which we get when we use the love of these significant people to glimpse and grasp Jesus' love in a way that engages our whole person, our body, soul and heart as well as our mind. (Lk 10:25-28)

If you want to draw fruit from the mysteries of Christ's

life, you must offer yourself as present to whatever was said or done through our Lord Jesus Christ with the whole affective power of your mind, with loving care, with lingering delight; thus laying aside all other worries and cares . *(Ludolf of Saxony)*

Getting our whole person involved

The Spirit leads us into an interior knowledge of Jesus' love and its glory by engaging our whole person in it. In other words, the gospel stories, like our own and those of others, engage our senses as we listen to and savour what Jesus says and does in them. These stories also engage our soul in giving us an intuitive glimpse of the way Jesus relates or loves. This glimpse of Jesus' love is attractive and arouses feelings in us that need to be expressed. To be assured that we are loved by Jesus is so important that we are willing to work towards translating the glimpses we get of his love into the convictions of it we call faith.

We have a lot of experience of being loved by the significant people in our lives and this can be an asset or an encumbrance. It is an asset if we use this fund of experience of human love to make the love of Jesus and its beauty more real, colourful and engaging. It can also be an encumbrance in that the memory of people's love can put us in touch with its shortcomings, with how limited and wayward it often is. This experience of human love, often in a subconscious way, governs how we see and feel about Jesus. Therefore, if we are to benefit from our rich resource of human love, we need to cultivate it as an asset and also to become aware of how the limitations of those who have loved us can deter us from drawing on this rich resource.

Contemplating Jesus in a gospel story

In every gospel story the Spirit wants to give us a glimpse of Jesus' love and to attract us with its beauty so that our whole person is drawn to believe in it. For our part, we need to notice and put words on the aspect of Jesus' love and its attractiveness that the Spirit brings to our attention. We can then focus on savouring and gradually making our own of this love. The first preface of Christmas succinctly expresses our longing to see this vision of Jesus and to be enraptured by it.

In the wonder of the Incarnation
your eternal Word has brought to the eyes of faith
a new and radiant vision of your glory.
In him we see our God made visible
and so are caught up in
(enraptured) love of the God we cannot see.

THE EXERCISE
The following is a practical way of contemplating Jesus in a gospel story so that we get an intimate knowledge of his love and get enraptured by or 'caught up in the love of the God we cannot see':

1 Quieten yourself in whatever way you wish, such as by listening to the sounds you hear around you. Then focus your attention on the desire of the Trinity to reveal themselves to you by repeating a word or phrase that helps you to do this.

2 Choose a story from the gospels in which you find a picture of Jesus that appeals to you. Read this and notice what aspect of Jesus' love it reveals to you. Choose a word or a phrase that captures for you the love revealed in the story.

3 Spend time letting the attractiveness of this aspect of Jesus' love grow. It may help to ponder the way someone you know radiates this kind of love.

4 Put words on what, in effect, Jesus is saying in this piece of scripture and then let him say these words to you. The more challenging and personal are the words you choose the better. Let Jesus say these words to you a number of times so that the love they express may sink in.

5 Tell Jesus how you feel about what he says to you. You may find that one part of you resists this while another part welcomes it with gratitude or joy.

CHAPTER 19

The Mass

The Holy Grail is the chalice and platter used by Christ at the Last Supper. It is kept in a castle whose king is unaware of its presence and as a result he is afflicted by a debilitating illness that nobody can heal. His whole kingdom shares the effects of his sickness and lies desolate.

In a remote part of the kingdom there lives a simple youth called Parsifal. On being trained as a knight he is given three rules to live by: he must not seduce or be seduced, he must seek the Holy Grail and an answer to the question, 'Whom does the Grail serve?' After many years on his journey he meets the king who invites him to his castle. Parsifal's visit to the castle is fruitless as he fails to recognise the Holy Grail and to ask the crucial question. So, the king is not healed and the land continues to be desolate.

Parsifal sets out on his journey again but allows himself to be seduced and diverted from his quest. Eventually he meets a hermit who absolves him and gives him instructions on where to find the Grail castle. When he finds it he asks the question, 'Whom does the Grail serve?', and receives the following answer, 'The Grail must serve the Grail King.' With Parsifal's help the king becomes aware of the presence of the Holy Grail and the need to be at the service of the love it represents. As a result, he and his kingdom are healed and their desolation gives way to joy as they learn to acknowledge the presence of the Holy Grail.

The Grail Legend is about life's main quest. For the Christian this is to know the love of Jesus, especially to know its greatest expression when Jesus loves us to 'the utmost extent'. It is to savour and assimilate this love that Jesus invites us to eat his body and to drink his blood at Mass.

'The Grail must serve the Grail King'

To appreciate the true meaning and beauty of the Mass we must learn to see it in the context of the passionate desire of the persons of the Trinity to reveal the full extent and depth of their love for us. All our energies and resources must be put at the service of this for it is in this sense that 'The Grail must serve the Grail King'. This reality of their love and our lovableness in their eyes must be kept alive at all costs, for if it is not, we, like the king and his people, remain debilitated and desolate. The book of Wisdom confronts us with the danger of forgetting and thus getting cut of from this vision of God's love when it says, '… lest falling into deep forgetfulness we get cut off from your kindness'. (Wis 16:12)

> Among all my patients in the second half of life – that is to say over thirty five – there has not been one whose problem in the last resort was not that of finding a religious outlook on life. It is safe to say that every one of them fell ill because he had lost what the living religions of every age have given to their followers, and none of them has really been healed who did not regain his religious outlook. *(Carl Jung)*

Keeping the vision alive

By re-enacting his death and resurrection for us in the Mass, Jesus keeps before us a vision of his love of us 'to the utmost extent' and the awesome beauty of this. By remembering and savouring this at Mass we give ourselves time to be 'grasped' or captivated as Paul was by its attractiveness. 'I want to know Christ and the power of his resurrection … I press on to grasp ever more firmly that purpose for which Christ Jesus grasped me.' (Phil 3:10-12) Nothing is as powerful as the Mass for realising all that our baptism makes us capable of. 'The proper effect of the Eucharist is the transformation of a person into God.' (Thomas Aquinas)

The vision that must inspire our worship

Mass has for a long time now been seen as primarily worship, as something we do for God. In fact it is primarily something God does for us, a vision that results from God's self-revelation in Jesus' love of us 'to the utmost extent'. (Jn 13:1) It is the radiance of this love that must inspire our worship if it is to remain meaningful and to engage our whole person. It is this vision of the extraordinary beauty of the love of Jesus that makes the Mass such an extraordinary act of worship. It is this vision also that inspires us to say with passionate conviction, 'It is right and fitting that always and everywhere we should give you thanks and praise through Jesus Christ our Lord'. (Preface of the Mass) However, if this vision of God's love, that the Spirit wants to give us an intimate knowledge of at Mass, is not constantly renewed then the meaning and beauty of the Mass will wane and our worship will lose much of what is meant to inspire it.

The Mass as a dialogue that leads to union

The wondrous interplay of God's love and our Spirit-inspired worship forms the basis of the dialogue the Mass essentially is. In this dialogue we listen to God' self revelation in three places: in the readings, in the consecration and in the communion. To this revelation we respond in a corresponding three places: in the prayers that surround the consecration, in those that surround the communion but above all in the complete surrender of ourselves that we express in our offerings. The readings we find in the Word of God throughout the year tell the whole story of God's self revelation and the consecration is the climax of this story. The intense attractiveness of this vision of love that we see in the consecration draws us into the profound intimacy we celebrate in the communion of the Mass. Our worship is a response to this revelation of the love and glory of the risen Lord. In the prayers that surround the consecration and communion we voice our thanksgiving and praise as well as our dependence on God for all our needs. In our offering and in the prayers which surround it we express our willingness to 'repent and believe' in the love of Jesus that the Mass is the most profound expression of.

The communion in which Jesus wants us to abide

Jesus tells us that when he is 'lifted up' on the cross he will draw us to himself. 'And I, when I am lifted up from the earth, will draw all people (all things) to myself.' (Jn 12:32) The union we are drawn into is what we celebrate in the communion of the Mass. It is a share in the union which Jesus enjoys with his Father, a union Jesus speaks of as 'complete' when he prays that we 'may become completely one'. (Jn 17:22-23) This complete union is characterised by joy that is also complete. (Jn 17:13) And so we are invited to celebrate with a meal the union that the radiance of Jesus' love to the end draws us into. At this banquet the poet envisages each of us being attended to by Jesus.

> Love bade me welcome; yet my soul drew back,
> Guiltie of dust and sinne.
> But quick-ey'd Love, observing me grow slack
> From my first entrance in,
> Drew nearer to me, sweetly questioning,
> If I lack'd any thing.
>
> A guest I answer'd, worthy to be here:
> Love said, you shall be he.
> I the unkinde, ungrateful? Ah my deare,
> I cannot look on thee.
> Love took my hand, and smiling did reply,
> Who made the eyes but I? .
>
> Truth Lord, but I have marr'd them: let my shame
> Go where it doth deserve.
> And know you not, sayes Love, who bore the blame?
> My deare, then I will serve.
> You must sit down, says Love, and taste my meat:
> So I did sit and eat. *(George Herbert)*

AN EXERCISE: Take your favourite prayer from the Mass and after quietening your body and focusing your spirit, read the prayer as a whole. Then dwell with each phrase of it, saying each a number of times. Allow yourself time to savour its meaning and to express any feeling this gives rise to. Finally, say the whole prayer again and notice whether it has become more meaningful and engaging for you.

CHAPTER 20

The Spirit as our 'Advocate'

In the following poem William Shakespeare notices how he can be drawn down two very different roads. Which one he takes depends on whom he believes in and this is revealed to him by the way he feels.

Sonnet 29
When, in disgrace with fortune and in men's eyes,
I all alone beweep my outcast state,
And trouble deaf heaven with my bootless cries,
And look upon myself and curse my fate,
Wishing me like to one more rich in hope,
Featured like him, like him with friends possessed,
Desiring this man's art and that man's scope,
With what I most enjoy contented least;
Yet in these thoughts myself almost despising,
Haply I think on thee – and then my state,
Like to the lark at break of day arising,
From sullen earth, sings hymns at heaven's gate;
For thy sweet love rememb'red such wealth brings
That then I scorn to change my state with kings.

Two ways, two visions and two spirits
There are two spirits, the 'natural' and the 'spiritual', at work in each of us leading us along two very different ways. 'The natural person has no room for the gifts of God's Spirit; to him they are folly; he cannot recognise them, because their value can be assessed only in the Spirit. The spiritual person, on the other hand, can assess the value of everything … but we are those who have the mind of Christ.' (1 Cor 2:14-18)

So, as well as being our teacher who shapes our vision, the Spirit helps us to 'assess the value of everything' and as a result we can discern what ways of acting are in keeping with what is important for us or not. In this way the Spirit helps us to discern between what Jesus in his parable of the two ways calls the 'broad way that leads to destruction' and 'the narrow way that leads to life'. (Mt 7:13-14) The story of Rapunzel provides a key to understanding the influences at work on us when we choose one of these roads rather than the other.

There was once this little girl called Rapunzel who was very beautiful. She was captured by a witch who realised that to hold on to Rapunzel she had to convince her that she was ugly. If she knew she was beautiful she would go off with one of the young men who came to consult the witch. If, on the other hand, she was convinced she was ugly she would be afraid of being seen by them and would therefore hide when they were around. So the witch gradually convinced Rapunzel that she was ugly and thereafter when anyone came to the witch's house she hid for fear of being seen.

One day when she was combing her hair in her room, she became conscious of someone looking at her through the window. Instinctively she looked up. Then she saw, in the eyes of the young man gazing at her, that she was beautiful. Gradually, as she learned to believe this, her fear was replaced by joy. She set off on the long journey of freeing herself from the deadening influence of the witch to accept the life and happiness offered to her by the young man's love.

We have a strong tendency to believe the witch and to accept a harmful illusion about ourselves. Even though the weak and wayward side of us is only a fraction of who we are, we tend to see it as much bigger than this. The signs of our limitations tend, like a black spot on a sheet of white paper, to fix our attention. The negative side of ourselves can dominate what we see and obscure the vision God wants us to believe in. It is this vision rather than people or circumstances that determines how happy we are.

Like the winds of the sea are the ways of fate
As we voyage along through life.

'Tis the set of a soul that decides its goal,
And not the calm or the strife.

How the two spirits influence us

The story of Rapunzel can help us to be more aware of how the
two spirits influence us. Rapunzel is invited to choose between
two visions of herself and two sets of feelings generated by these
two visions. Similarly, we have to choose who and what to believe in, the bad spirit who portrayed Rapunzel as ugly, or the
good spirit represented by the young man who invited Rapunzel
to believe that she was beautiful. Which voice we choose to listen to and believe in will induce either positive or negative feelings. The positive feelings, such as joy and enthusiasm, are
based on faith, hope and love and form the basis of a life lived in
consolation. 'May the God of hope fill you with all joy and peace
in believing, so that you may abound in hope by the power of
the Holy Spirit.' (Rom 15:13)

The growth of a destructive illusion

It is our basic tragedy that we believe voices other than that of
the Spirit. Like Rapunzel we succumb to the illusion that we are
insignificant and not of much worth and to the persistent feelings of guilt, sadness and isolation that accompany this illusion.
Unaware of where this way of seeing and feeling is leading us
we take the way to 'destruction'. These negative feelings are
painful as they put us in touch with our inadequacy. To counter-
act this we try to prove our worth by our achievements, by what
we possess and by the work we do. The acclaim we achieve in
this way is superficial and short lived and eventually leads to
frustration and anxiety. Periodic feelings of sadness, guilt or
frustration are part of every life but when they become pro-
longed or excessive they are signs that we are under the dominance of the bad spirit. 'Now the Spirit expressly says that in later
times some will renounce the faith by paying attention to deceit-
ful spirits.' (1 Tim 4:1)

Being led along the way to life

We are led by the Spirit to take the narrow and more difficult
road to 'life' and we take this way when we believe and hope in

the love the Spirit plants in our hearts. (Rom 5:1-5, Jude 1:20-21) This is the love of God Jesus reveals to us or 'the mind of Christ' which the Spirit cultivates in us. (1 Cor 2:18) It is a vision of our-selves as loved and lovable that the Spirit helps us adopt by inviting us to notice and own the glimpses we are given of it. This growing belief that we are loved, to the degree Jesus tells us we are, produces a range of good feeling of which joy and peace are central. Paul describes a wide range of these feelings which he calls 'the fruit of the Spirit': '... the fruit of the Spirit is love, joy, peace, patience, kindness, generosity, faithfulness, gentle-ness, and self-control.' (Gal 5:22-23) 'I therefore, the prisoner in the Lord, beg you to lead a life worthy of the calling to which you have been called, with all humility and gentleness, with pat-ience, bearing with one another in love, making every effort to maintain the unity of the Spirit in the bond of peace.' (Eph 4:1-3)

> Yet in these thoughts myself almost despising,
> Haply I think on thee – and then my state,
> Like to the lark at break of day arising,
> From sullen earth, sings hymns at heaven's gate;
> For thy sweet love rememb'red such wealth brings
> That then I scorn to change my state with kings.
> *(William Shakespeare)*

AN EXERCISE: Read the story of Rapunzel again and notice if you can identify with what it is saying. Become aware of the signs of two influences at work on you in the form of the nega-tive and positive feelings that you are familiar with. Name some of these feelings that are prominent in your experience. Are there positive and negative ways of seeing yourself and others that you associate with each of these two kinds of feeling? Spend some time with the Spirit as the one who wants to make you more aware of who is leading you in life and of the supreme love and lovableness you are being led into. Rom 5:5, Jn 16:13 and 2 Cor 3:18 might help to assure you of this.

CHAPTER 21

The Fellowship of the Spirit

When twins, born prematurely, were put into separate incubators one of them thrived but the other deteriorated. When there was little hope for the survival of the weaker one, a nurse decided to put them side by side in a single incubator. When she returned after some time she found the stronger twin had put his arm around the weaker one who, to her amazement, began to thrive from then on.

A lifelong need
All through our lives we need an arm around us, a caring environment or a place where we are secure, accepted, affirmed and thus made feel significant. Our parents, by the love they give us, initially create this environment and it is as strong, extensive and permanent as their love. It is, however important that our parents give us wings as well as roots. When we do take wing we become responsible for maintaining and extending our caring environment as we always remain dependent on it for our growth. Creating a new environment or extending it involves leaving a place we are familiar with and comfortable in. We are like the crab that every so often must break the shell it has outgrown if it is to develop. As well as leaving home to establish, expand and maintain our own holding environment we need to return to the foundation on which this was initially built. We do this by returning to or remembering the love we have received from the significant people in our story.

In the film, *Cinema Paradiso*, Toto returns home after thirty years for the funeral of his friend Alfredo. Toto has become a famous film director and has many admiring fans but he has forgotten and got cut off from the love of those who cared for him during his early years. He now realises that he has 'abandoned' his mother and that he has been abandoned by the girl who was his first love. He also failed to keep in touch with Alfredo who as a true friend had urged him to leave home in order to fulfil his dream. After the funeral Toto returns to Rome a much happier person for he has been in touch again with the people who made and sustained him and will now hopefully continue to do so.

The fellowship of the Spirit

In the introductory prayers of the Mass the environment created by the love of God poured into our hearts is called 'the fellowship of the Spirit'. 'The grace of the Lord Jesus Christ, the love of God and the fellowship of the Holy Spirit be with you all.' (2 Cor 13:14) In scripture the term 'fellowship' is often used for the union with his Father that Jesus draws us into; a union characterised by a joy. 'We declare to you what we have seen and heard so that you also may have fellowship with us; and truly our fellowship is with the Father and with his Son Jesus Christ. We are writing these things so that our joy may be complete.' (1 Jn 1:3)

This fellowship is based on the fact that we have 'become participants of the divine nature' (2 Pet 1:4) and it is the Spirit who builds this environment or place where we dwell with God. 'In Christ you also are built together in the Spirit into a dwelling place for God'. (Eph 2:22) It is also the Spirit who through baptism incorporates us into Christ so that we can be with him before his Father. 'For just as the body is one and has many members, and all the members of the body, though many, are one body, so it is with Christ. For in the one Spirit we were all baptised into one body.' (1 Cor 12:12-13) This influence of the Spirit makes itself felt in our spirit but also in our body which becomes the temple of the Spirit. 'Or do you not know that your body is a temple of the Holy Spirit within you, which you have from God, and that you are not your own? For you were bought with a price; therefore glorify God in your body.' (1 Cor 6:19-20) It is the Spirit who initiates and sustains the dialogue going on within this home we have with God, enabling us to say with Jesus from deep within it, 'Abba! Father!' 'And because you are children, God has sent the Spirit of his Son into our hearts, crying, 'Abba! Father!' (Gal 4:6)

A union in which everything is shared
Jesus speaks of our fellowship with him in terms of friendship. He understands this friendship in a uniquely profound way as for him it is based on sharing with each person 'everything' he has and is; this involves sharing with us his own relationship with his Father. 'I have called you friends, because I have made known to you everything that I have heard from my Father.' (Jn 15:15) Since the Spirit proceeds from the Father and the Son and personifies and epitomises their love and union, it is the Spirit who gives us an interior knowledge of 'everything' Jesus and the Father share.

What characterises the fellowship of the Spirit
We will conclude this chapter by looking at four characteristics of the fellowship we enjoy with the persons of the Trinity. We examined these four in detail in chapters 5-11 so we will focus here on outlining the Spirit's role in fostering them in the fellowship or holding environment the Spirit surrounds us with. This is an environment in which our deepest dream is fulfilled or in which the beauty of the Spirit's love draws us into an intimate union permeated with joy.

> And the most blessed Trinity, in its unity, took hold of my soul like a thing that belonged to it and that it had made capable of receiving its divine impression and the effects of its divine interchange ... From that time onwards, the effects took root and, as the three divine Persons possessed me, so did I possess them too. (*Marie of the Incarnation*)

The Spirit's dream for us
Just as any environment is as strong, intimate and personal as the love that creates and sustains it, that of the Spirit is as strong, intimate and personal as the love of God which the Spirit pours into our hearts and constantly leads us into. (Rom 5:5, Jn 16:13) As well as leading us into the full extent and depth of Jesus' love the Spirit highlights the attractiveness of this love or the glory that radiates from it. (2 Cor 3:18) The effect of this intense attractiveness of Jesus is that it draws us into a union with him so that we become one with him before the Father. (Jn 12:32) Therefore, under the influence of the Spirit we cry out with Jesus, 'Abba!

Father!' (Rom 8:14-17) This union or environment we now live in is permeated with a joy we experience 'in the Holy Spirit.' 'For the kingdom of God is not food and drink but righteousness and peace and joy in the Holy Spirit.' (Rom 14:17)

How much the Holy Spirit pervades the environment we live in is beautifully portrayed in the following prayer of St Fursa who lived in Ireland in the 7th century. The lorica that gives its name to his prayer is like a breastplate worn to protect one's body, but being made of leather it provides an intimate, supple and warm environment for the wearer. As such it is a symbol of how the Spirit's love provides the environment which nurtures us.

The Lorica of St Fursa (7th C)
The arm of God be around my shoulders,
  the touch of the Holy Spirit upon my head,
  the sign of Christ's cross be upon my forehead,
  the sound of the Holy Spirit in my ears,
  the fragrance of the Holy Spirit in my nostrils,
  the vision of heaven's company in my eyes,
  the conversation of heaven's company on my lips,
  the work of God's church in my hands,
  the service of God and the neighbour in my feet,
  a home for God in my heart,
  and to God, the Father of all, my entire being. Amen

AN EXERCISE: Reflect on your experience of someone who provided or provides a holding or caring environment for you to live in. As you reflect on this person's love and the atmosphere that remembering it revives, notice how you see and feel about it now. Meet the Holy Spirit and after being quiet in each other's presence, begin a dialogue in which you talk about what characterises the environment the Spirit seeks to build around you. At the end of the conversation write down what you see and feel as a result of it. Conclude by praying the Lorica of St Fursa.

PART 4

Introduction

The Seven Gifts of the Spirit enable us to be sensitive and responsive to the love that the Spirit pours into our hearts. They help us to be sensitive to the way the Spirit leads us into this love by enlightening our minds. They also help us to be responsive to the way the Spirit highlights the radiance of this love so that we may be drawn to believe in it. Three of the gifts give us a heightened sense of the extent, depth and all-pervasive nature of the Spirit's love. The other four make us responsive to the attractiveness or glory emanating from this love so that we may 'abide in' or get our whole person involved in owning it.

The chapters in Part 4 focus initially on the history and nature of the Seven Gifts. Then we devote a chapter to each one of them. *Understanding* keeps us in touch with the big picture of what Jesus calls the 'good news' and with how everything in life is part of this. *Wisdom* involves getting an in-depth appreciation of what is most important in life as this gives all else meaning and worth. *Knowledge* finds that all things are signs of, and thus put us in touch with, what is central to life. *Fear of the Lord* governs our basic response to God being both transcendent and immanent, being Lord as well as Lover. *Piety* enables us to immerse ourselves in the reality of God being Lover and Lord so that we surrender to him our whole person, body and soul, mind and heart. *Fortitude* gives us the courage to face the forces inside and outside ourselves that make it difficult for us to believe that God is Lover and Lord. *Counsel* enables us to discern in concrete situations how to live consistently with what we believe in.

The Seven Gifts of the Holy Spirit

Make us sensitive and responsive
to the Spirit's enlightenment and attraction

Three gifts make us sensitive to the Spirit's enlightenment:

> Understanding: seeing the big picture

> Wisdom: what is at the centre, holding all together

> Knowledge: how everything is a sign of what is at the centre

Four gifts make us responsive to the Spirit's attraction:

> Fear of the Lord: living with God being Lord and Lover

> Piety: involving our whole person in response to this

> Fortitude: the courage this calls for

> Counsel: discerning how to live consistently with this vision

Seven Gifts of the Spirit

The film *Regarding Henry* starts off with a portrait of Henry as a very aggressive lawyer who dominates the lives of those who work for him. Then in a mugging incident he is so badly injured that he forgets who he is and has to discover this again. Gradually he begins to piece together his past and does not like the picture he finds of his former self. So he sets about trying to change and a whole new Henry begins to emerge, one who is much more human than the original person.

There is much resistance to these changes among the people Henry works with as his old self fitted in much better in the law firm in which he works. The firm starts to exclude him when he tries to undo some of his injustices to people he had prosecuted. His wife and daughter, whom he hardly knew before the accident, now become the centre of his life and in his relationship with them he discovers a whole new self that he is very content to be.

When, like Henry, we focus on meeting the expectations of our outer world we tend to neglect the basic relationships that are central to our inner one. The Seven Gifts of the Holy Spirit are given to enable us to tune in to our inner world, to find again the relationships that must be our priority in life. In practice, the Seven Gifts enable us to develop our relationships by enabling us to listen and respond to God, to ourselves, to others and to all things; these relationships will be as good as this ability to communicate.

Where do the Seven Gifts come from?
The scriptural source of the gifts is Isaiah 11:1-2 where it says, 'A shoot shall come out from the stump of Jesse, and a branch shall

grow out of his roots. The spirit of the Lord shall rest on him, the spirit of wisdom and understanding, the spirit of counsel and might, the spirit of knowledge and piety and he will be filled with the spirit of the fear of the Lord.' The Jerusalem Bible comments as follows on these verses: 'The prophetic spirit confers on the Messiah the outstanding virtues of his great ancestors: the wisdom and insight of Solomon and the heroism and prudence of David, the knowledge and fear of God characteristic of patriarch and prophet, of Moses, of Jacob, of Abraham.'

How the Seven Gifts developed

Yves Congar in his book, *I Believe in the Holy Spirit*, says that Thomas Aquinas elaborated on the role given to these Gifts in 1235 by Philip the Chancellor. In his teaching Thomas returns repeatedly to Rom 8:14, as the predominant idea in his theology is that only God can lead us into the place where he dwells, into the divine milieu. 'For all who are led by the Spirit of God are children of God ... When we cry, "Abba! Father!" it is that very Spirit bearing witness with our spirit that we are children of God, and if children, then heirs with Christ.' (Rom 8:14-17) Congar goes on to say: 'The gifts of the Spirit are distinct from the virtues because they make the practice of the latter perfect. They are those permanent dispositions which make the Christian ... ready to follow the movement of divine inspiration or the Holy Spirit ... We are led by another, who does not act without us and does not use violence, but who nonetheless goes beyond anything we can see or expect.' The Spirit goes beyond not only our views and expectations based on human reason, but also those that come from faith. 'What no eye has seen, nor ear heard, nor the human heart conceived, what God has prepared for those who love him' – these things God has revealed to us through the Spirit; for the Spirit searches everything, even the depths of God ... And we speak of these things in words not taught by human wisdom but taught by the Spirit, interpreting spiritual things to those who are spiritual.' (1 Cor 2:9-13)

The Gifts, the Virtues, the Beatitudes and Fruit of the Spirit

For Thomas, the gifts are not superior to the theological virtues but enable us to practise these virtues perfectly. Thomas, following 'a great spiritual tradition', links the gifts with the virtues and with the beatitudes which he sees as their 'perfect action'. For example, he links Understanding (inner penetration) with faith and with 'the pure in heart', However relative these correspondences are, and their basis in scripture, there is, according to Balthasar, a 'great tradition of weaving the virtues, the gifts, the beatitudes and the fruit of the Spirit into a spiritual synthesis. Thomas is to the fore in this integration of the gifts into the fabric of his detailed analysis of the virtues throughout the Summa.'

Thomas also devoted space in his Summa to the 'fruit of the Spirit', which he saw as 'the ultimate and delightful product of the action of the Holy Spirit in us'. Fruit is the ultimate product of the plant and good to taste. The 'fruit of the Spirit' (Gal 5:22) can also be called 'the harvest of the Spirit'. This harvest is basically love, of which 'joy, peace, patience, kindness, goodness, faithfulness, gentleness and self-control' are an unfolding. These and similar lists in Paul are an ideal portrait of the Christian and of the love described in 1 Cor 13:4-7. Jesus, as 'meek and humble of heart', epitomises this picture of the quiet goodness and beauty of the best people we know.

> I say more, the just man justices;
> Keeps grace: that keeps all his goings graces;
> Acts in God's eye what in God's eye he is –
> Christ. For Christ plays in ten thousand places,
> Lovely in limbs, and lovely in eyes not his
> To the Father through the features of men's faces.
> (G. M. Hopkins)

An instinct for life within the Trinity

Though Balthasar, in his book *The Spirit of Truth,* does not deal with the seven gifts individually, he believes that the work of the Spirit is treated by the Middle Ages as one of guiding us into an interior knowledge of the love Jesus expresses in human terms. (1 Cor 2:12) 'This whole work of "guiding" us into the divine nature, including everything that, in the school of Bernard, is described as "tasting and knowing things from within" is unambiguously in the service of understanding Jesus. For Thomas the Seven Gifts, that he sets forth with such genius, all serve to infuse into our cognitive powers an *instinctus* that operates by divine love.'

The Gifts give us an instinct or feeling for the new order established by our becoming participants in the divine nature. (2 Pet 1:4) They enable us to cry out, 'Abba Father!' (Gal:4:6) and to be receptive and responsive to this wondrous relationship we are called into. It is a relationship that has its roots in the love the Spirit pours into our heart, in the faith that makes us receptive to this love and in the hope that makes us responsive to it. (1 Cor 2:9-10) The seven gifts are, thus, at the service of faith, hope and love. Three of the gifts, Understanding, Wisdom and Knowledge, are at the service of faith and help us to listen and be receptive to the way the Spirit opens up her love for us by enlightening us. The four remaining gifts, Fear of the Lord, Piety, Fortitude and Counsel, are at the service of hope, and help us to respond to the attractiveness of the love the Spirit opens up for us. These gifts give us a feeling for 'the dearest freshness deep down things' of a new dawn.

> And for all this, nature is never spent;
> There lives the dearest freshness deep down things;
> And though the last lights of the black West went
> Oh, morning, at the brown brink eastward, springs –
> Because the Holy Ghost over the bent
> World broods with warm breast and with ah! bright wings.
> (G. M. Hopkins)

AN EXERCISE: The people living the Christian life to the full are often quietly loving. They exercise their art of loving with such masterly ease that we may not notice how beautiful they are until we reflect on their lives after they have died. Recall such a person from your experience and notice and name the way the fruit of the Spirit's love, listed in Gal 5:22 and in 1 Cor 13:4-7, becomes evident to you in this person's life. Now notice and appreciate some of these same qualities in your own way of relating.

The Gift of Understanding

The Stork
A man, who lived by a pond, was awakened one night by an unusual noise. Though it was snowing, he went out into the night and not being sure where the noise was coming from, he walked up and down, back and forth until he eventually found a leak in the wall of the pond from which water and fish were escaping. He set to work plugging the leak and then went back to bed. The next morning, looking out from second floor window of his house, he saw to his surprise that his footprints had traced the figure of what seemed to him like a stork.

We live our lives twice, the first time round we experience the people and events of our life as they occur. Then at some stage we may look back in a reflective way on what has happened and discover that there is a pattern in our experience, a pattern symbolised by the stork the man had traced by his footsteps in the snow. It is the Spirit's gift of Understanding that helps us to see the pattern woven out of the multiplicity of events that make up our lives. It enables us to put together the pieces of the jigsaw puzzle so that an overall picture emerges. Each of us has a lot of experience that we are unaware of and have never integrated to form a meaningful whole. What causes our experience to remain unintegrated is that we lose touch with the centre that holds everything together and gives it meaning and value. 'Things fall apart' when this centre no longer holds.

Turning and turning in the widening gyre
The falcon cannot hear the falconer;
Things fall apart; the centre cannot hold;
Mere anarchy is loosed upon the world. *(W. B. Yeats)*

When the prodigal son leaves his father and goes into a far country he separates himself from the person whose care has made and sustained him. (Lk 15:11-32) We in our turn go into a far country in search of pleasure and status as well as the work and wealth that provide us with these. When we become preoccupied with these outer things we leave little time for the inner world of relationships and the love we receive and return within them. We no longer remember and so get cut off from the care and 'kindness' that make us who we are. '... falling into deep forgetfulness we get cut off from your kindness'. (Wis 16:12) It is as if we live in the cellar of a very beautiful house every inch of which God wants us to enjoy. We experience the tragedy Shirley faced in the film *Shirley Valentine* when she realised she had lived the 'little life' of meeting endless expectations and had neglected her dream of being Shirley Valentine.

> I've led such a little life, and even that will be over pretty soon
> I've allowed myself to lead this little life,
> when inside me there is so much more, and it's all gone unused
> And now it never will be.
> Why do we get all this life if we never use it?
> Why do we get all these feelings, and dreams and hopes?
> That's where Shirley Valentine disappeared.

Jesus seeks to liberate us from the small world we allow ourselves be confined in. At the beginning of Luke's gospel we hear him say: 'The Spirit of the Lord is upon me, because he has anointed me to bring good news to the poor. He has sent me to proclaim release to the captives and recovery of sight to the blind, to let the oppressed go free, to proclaim the year of the Lord's favour.' (Lk 4:18)

> As someone previously in darkness, suddenly seeing the sun, receives sight and sees clearly what he did not see before, so those deemed worthy of the Holy Spirit are enlightened in soul and see beyond the power of human sight what they did not know before. (*St Cyril of Jerusalem*)

Jesus does not want us to become confined to the boundaries of our outer world but to live in the unlimited inner world of his love and the relationships this love draws us into. He wants us to discover the beautiful design he is weaving out of all that happens to us in life.

Letting the love of Jesus mould our mind and heart
At the centre of this vision of our inner world, giving all meaning and worth, is the love of the Father that Jesus and the Spirit reveal to us. Paul prays that we 'may be strengthened in our inner being with power through his Spirit ... to know the love of Christ that surpasses knowledge.' (Eph 3:16-19) Jesus makes this love known in each gospel story where he gives a vision that satisfies more than our mind as it is a vision of a love that is radiant and beautiful. As we learn to perceive this vision it engages our whole person and enraptures us with its beauty. (Phil 3:10-12) We are drawn to Jesus in such a way that the attractiveness of his love creates a magnetic field within which everything in us and around us is re-ordered in relation to him. 'And I, when I am lifted up from the earth, will draw all people (all things) to myself.' (Jn 12:32) The nearest comparable human experience to this is what happens to two people when they fall in love. They begin to centre their lives on their beloved, viewing and valuing everything in relation to this person. This new order created by Jesus' love, in which everyone and everything has its place, is like the pattern or big picture that is created when all the pieces of the jigsaw puzzle are in place.

'Love one another as I have loved you'
The Spirit's gift of Understanding helps us to find what is central to life and to see all else in relationship to this. It helps us find the stork, the pattern, the big picture that the pieces of jigsaw fit together to form. Finding this pattern of the stork in life's footprints involves becoming increasingly aware of three things: Jesus' love of us, its glory and the fellowship this love and glory draw us into.

Firstly, Understanding makes us increasingly sensitive to the Spirit's enlightenment, to how we are being led to see a vision of the length and breadth of Jesus' love. (Jn 16:13, Eph 3:18-19) According as this vision of Jesus clarifies, we are drawn to see everything in relation to it, as a person who is in love finds everything that receives its meaning in relationship to the person he or she loves.

Secondly, the gift of Understanding makes us sensitive to the way the Spirit attracts us with the radiance of Jesus' love. The intense attractiveness of this love keeps our heart fixed on Jesus as what we value most. From this allure of Jesus' love we get the energy to change our mind and heart to believe the good news and to value everything in its light.

Thirdly, by leading us into Jesus' love and its beauty, the Spirit draws us into a network of relationships based on Jesus' commandment that we love others and all creation as he has loved us. Through the gift of Understanding the Spirit 'teaches us everything' or how everything fits together in God's grand design for our lives. 'But the Advocate, the Holy Spirit, whom the Father will send in my name, will teach you everything, and remind you of all that I have said to you.' (Jn 14:26)

> Look, as your looking-glass by chance may fall,
> Divide, and break in many pieces small
> And yet shows forth the self-same face in all,
>
> Proportions, features, graces, just the same,
> And in the smallest piece as well the name
> Of fairest one deserves as in the richest frame.
>
> So all my thoughts are pieces of you,
> Which put together make a glass so true
> As I therein no other's face but yours can view.
> *(Michael Drayton)*

AN EXERCISE: Make a list of the different areas of your experience, such as family, work, leisure. Then put your more important ones in the centre of a page. Finally, select the most important area and then notice how it gives meaning and value to all the rest of your experience.

CHAPTER 24

The Gift of Wisdom

In Tolstoy's novel *War and Peace*, Pierre discovered in his wife's love for him something lovable and even glorious about himself. In an earlier marriage he had experienced how fickle his own love was. It was as if his present wife held up a mirror before him, one in which he saw in a mysterious way his own goodness.

After seven years of married life, Pierre had a firm and joyful consciousness that he was not a bad fellow, and he felt this because he saw himself reflected in his wife. In himself he felt all the good and bad mingled together and obscuring one another. But in his wife he saw reflected only what was really good; everything not quite good was left out. And this result was reached, not by way of logical reflection but by way of a mysterious, direct reflection of himself. *(Tolstoy, War and Peace.)*

There is a shift of focus here in Pierre's life that often occurs in our middle years. It is a shift from an outer to an inner world, from a world in which what we do and what we have are a priority, to a world in which our relationships are central. From an early age there is much we have learned about these relationships and about the love we receive and give within them. However, we are not conscious of this accumulation of inner wisdom until circumstances challenge us to draw on the resources we have in this stream of inner wisdom.

Our underground stream of inner wisdom
Well below the surface of our lives there is a stream of inner wisdom. It runs underground because we do not take the trouble to become conscious of it. It is a stream of unique experience that runs from one end of life to the other and because it is so personal

no one else has access to it. The inner wisdom we find in this stream is the accumulated experience of our relationships and the love we have received and returned within them. What makes it an inner wisdom as opposed to an outer one is the fact that it is derived from our unique experience of the four levels at which we carry on our relationships. To access our inner wisdom we need to begin by recalling the story of the significant people and events in our lives and then seek to understand their significance. The feelings which the memory of significant people and events arouse make an important contribution to our wisdom if they are noticed and expressed. However, the most important part of our inner wisdom is our convictions about what is true and worthwhile in life. These convictions form the vision and the values that give everything its meaning and value.

The eyes are blind; one must listen with the heart
The Spirit's gift of Wisdom offers us an interior knowledge of what is central to the big picture that the gift of Understanding opens up for us. Whereas the gift of Understanding gives us a vision of the 'length and breadth' of Jesus' love the gift of Wisdom gives us a vision of its 'height and depth'. (Eph 3:18-19) This vision is revealed to us in all its splendour when Jesus, in his death and resurrection, loves us 'to the utmost extent'. In other words, Wisdom is encapsulated in the vision of Christ crucified.

> He kneeled long
> And saw love in a dark crown
> Of thorns blazing, a winter tree
> Golden with fruit of a man's body.
> (R. S. Thomas)

At the heart of the gift of Wisdom is an interior knowledge of Jesus' love and of the love of all those people who have made his love real for us. Along with love, Wisdom also gives us an interior knowledge of the glory, union and joy that love leads us into. Wisdom thus helps us to realise the Spirit's dream for us, the dream described in all its splendour by Jesus in chapter 17 of John's gospel.

Wisdom as a vision that enraptures us

The gift of Wisdom, in opening up for us a vision of Jesus' love, opens up a vision of its radiance or glory. This is a vision not just of Jesus' love and its beauty but of our own lovableness and glory in Jesus' eyes. Throughout life we are being led by the Spirit into a realisation that we are 'being transfigured in ever-increasing splendour into the image of Jesus and that this is the work of the Lord, the Spirit'. (2 Cor 3:18)

> The glory of God is a person fully alive
> The glory of a person is the vision of God.
> *(St Irenaeus)*

A fellowship and its joy known from the inside

Besides the love and glory the Spirit's gift of Wisdom opens up for us there is an intimate experience of the union that this love and glory draw us into. This is the union Jesus talks about when he says, 'And I, when I am lifted up from the earth, will draw all people (all things) to myself.' (Jn 12:32) In another place he says that the radiance of the love, that his death and resurrection reveals, 'gathers into one the dispersed children of God'. (Jn 11:52) What we are drawn into is an intimate experience of the life of God from the inside, an experience based on our 'participation in the divine nature'. (2 Pet 1:4) We are so much part of the life of Jesus that, inspired by the Spirit, we can say with him 'Abba! Father!' 'For all who are led by the Spirit of God are children of God. When we cry, "Abba! Father!" it is that very Spirit bearing witness with our spirit that we are children of God, and if children, then heirs, heirs of God and joint heirs with Christ.' (Rom 8:14-17)

Inseparable from the union with the Trinity we are called into, is the joy that permeates it. This joy, also called peace and happiness in the Bible, is an essential part of the love that Wisdom opens up before us. (Jn 15:9-11) Paul believes that this 'peace and joy' pervades the kingdom of God, or the whole environment that the love of Jesus draws us into. 'For the kingdom of God is not food and drink but righteousness and peace and joy in the Holy Spirit.' (Rom 14:17)

Down to earth Wisdom

There is a danger that we may see the gift of Wisdom as dealing with matters too exalted and spiritual to be part of our messy world. When this happens, Wisdom fails to engage us and so it becomes a part of our dormant experience. However, Jesus makes this gift very real and relevant when he says, 'This is my commandment, that you love one another as I have loved you.' (Jn 15:12) The primary meaning of this commandment is to be found in the vision it gives us of how deeply loved we are and how glorious this makes us. According as we accept this reality we will be enabled to see how lovable and glorious is the life of every person we meet. We will also know what kind of behaviour is consistent with this vision of ourselves and others since everyone becomes the person for whom Christ died and must be treated as such.

> All but a scattered few, live out their time,
> Husbanding that which they possess within,
> And go to the grave unthought-of. Strongest minds
> Are often those of whom the noisy world
> Hears least.
> *(William Wordsworth)*

Understanding, Wisdom and Knowledge

The gift of Wisdom gives us an intimate knowledge of the love that is central to the overall picture of our lives that the gift of Understanding opens up before us. The gift of Knowledge, we now move on to look at, enables us to see everything in creation as a sign of the love which the Spirit 'pours into our hearts'; thus everything can put us in touch with God.

AN EXERCISE: Read again the piece about how Pierre gained an important insight into his life and then recall a time in your own life when you got a similar insight. Sketch the story of this insight, what led up to it and what it has meant to you since. Notice and express any feelings this arouses. After reflecting on what you have written enter a dialogue with the Spirit and continue this until both of you have said all you want to say.

The Gift of Knowledge

St Bruno and the Bullfrog

The Prayer of St Bruno was interrupted by the croaking of the bullfrog. When he could stand it no longer, he shouted out the window, 'Would you please be quiet! I am trying to pray.' So all went quiet and Bruno settled down to pray. However, a voice inside him kept insisting, 'Perhaps the frog was praying too, and God may be as pleased with its prayer as with yours.'

When he could no longer gainsay the voice, Bruno ordered all the frogs to sing. From then on the song of the bullfrog never distracted him as he had learned not to fight the prayer of creation but to be in harmony with it. A world of prayer unlimited in its horizons opened up for Bruno.

Building bridges

The Spirit's gift of Knowledge enables us to find a bridge between the world of the bullfrogs and our prayer, between our outer, material world and our inner, spiritual one. This bridge, symbolised by the ladder in Jacob's dream, becomes a reality in the way Jesus connects the divine world and our human one. 'Very truly, I tell you, you will see heaven opened and the angels of God ascending and descending upon the Son of Man.' (Gen 28:10-22, Jn 1:51) This mutually enriching connection is established between the human and the divine when Jesus is formed by the Spirit in Mary. 'Joseph, son of David, do not be afraid to take Mary as your wife, for the child conceived in her is from the Holy Spirit.' (Mt 1:20)

Two attitudes to the material world

Two false attitudes to the world empty it of much of the meaning, value and beauty inherent in it. One of these attitudes distances us from the material world as it sees it as a source of temptation and even of evil. The other eroding attitude arises from the way science, economics and the consumer culture drains the material world of the significance and glory the Spirit gives to everything. The world is then seen in functional terms, as a resource to be exploited, rather than as a sacrament or as an outward sign revealing its caring creator.

> If your everyday life seems poor, don't
> blame it; blame yourself; admit to
> yourself that you are not enough of a poet
> to call forth its riches;
> *(Rainer Maria Rilke)*

Mutually enriching worlds
The Spirit's gift of Knowledge enables us to build a bridge between our material and spiritual worlds, between our body and our spirit. The two are inseparable from and dependent on each other. The material needs the spiritual to give it meaning and dignity whereas the spiritual needs the material to reveal itself to us and to make this revelation real, engaging and credible.

A love that gives meaning and value to all
When we are infants the love of our parents creates and sustains the caring environment we live in. As we grow up we become increasingly responsible for expanding and maintaining this environment by becoming more sensitive and responsive to the love on which the environment depends. The love which creates the environment in which Jesus wants us to live is, according to Jesus, the greatest possible love; it is so powerful that it draws everyone and everything not only to him but to each other as well. (Jn 15:13, 12:32) This is like the way a magnet creates a magnetic field within which everything, in being drawn to the magnet, is re-orientated within itself and with everything else within the magnetic field. In the new order or environment Jesus creates by his love of us 'to death' everyone becomes the person for whom he died and everything takes on a new sacredness. We 'are filled with all the fullness of God.' (Eph 3:19) and all creation 'is charged with the grandeur of God.' (G. M. Hopkins) The significance, the goodness and the beauty of everyone and everything

are increased in a way that cannot be measured. 'Earth's crammed with heaven and every bush afire with God.' (E. B. Browning)

The Smile of Jesus

If we but think what one human glance, one human smile, can do in our lives, how by such a smile we seem in a moment to be turned into a new man who in the strength of the love which comes to him in that small token can begin life anew, apparently with powers that were not there before – should we not be able to conceive how a smile of the man Jesus, God's smile, can change our life? And this is what the sacraments are, the God-Man's expression of love – with all its consequences. *(Edward Schillebeeckx, Christ The Sacrament)*

Seeing the significance and value that Jesus' love gives everything fosters an inclusive attitude like that which Peter was directed by the Spirit to adopt. 'The Spirit told me to go with them and not to make a distinction between them and us.' (Acts 11:12). Therefore, we need the gift of Knowledge to overcome our strong tendency to exclude from our relationships those who differ from us. It urges us to see the meaning and to appreciate the value of what we see around us, to constantly expand our horizons of what we see and are concerned about. This generates a growing sense of wonder and gratitude for the way our lives are blest by even the simplest of things.

Seeing with eyes the Spirit unsealed
Plough-horses in a quiet field.
(Patrick Kavanagh)

'This is the gate of heaven'

To the eyes that the Spirit's gift of Knowledge gives us, everyone and everything has its place on Jacob's ladder in that it reveals something about the wonder of God its creator and it can also prompt us to ascend the ladder in gratitude to God for it. Through the Spirit's gift of Knowledge we are inspired to notice and be in awe of God's presence in 'plough-horses in a quiet field' and to respond, like Jacob, in a moment of worship. 'Then Jacob woke from his sleep and said, 'Surely the Lord is in this place and I did not know it!' And he was afraid, and said, 'How awesome is this place! This is none other than the house of God, and this is the gate of heaven.' So Jacob rose early in the morning, and he took the stone that he had put under his head and set it up for a pillar and poured oil on the top of it. He called that place Bethel; That is House of God.' (Gen 28:16-19) The gift of Knowledge enables us to see the significance and the true value of each thing, to be grateful for the gift it is and to praise God, of whose love, presence and providence it is a wayside sacrament.

The angels keep their ancient places –
Turn but a stone and start a wing!
'Tis ye, 'tis your estranged faces,
That miss the many-splendoured thing.

But (when so sad thou canst not sadder)
Cry – and upon thy so sore loss
Shall shine the traffic of Jacob's ladder
Pitched betwixt Heaven and Charing Cross.
(Francis Thompson)

AN EXERCISE: Take an object, such as water, that you make use of daily and, after quietening yourself, name some of its uses. Imagine what life would be like without it and how you would manage. Allow yourself to get in touch with the wonder of water and read Jacob's prayer in Genesis 28:10-19. Say your own prayer of praise and gratitude for this gift or sign from God of his providence.

The Gift of Fear

Taking time to sharpen the saw

At the end of his book, *Seven Habits of Highly Effective People*, Stephen Covey gives the following illustration of a choice that is always confronting us. He asks us to imagine ourselves walking in a forest and coming across a forester culling trees. After watching him for some time we become aware that his saw is not very sharp, for though he is working hard he is not making much progress. During a break he takes from his work we remark on the fact that his saw does not seem to be sharp enough. He anticipates our suggestion that he should take time to sharpen his saw with the words, 'I don't have time to sharpen the saw for I must get this job finished before nightfall.'

Many things compete for space in our lives, for the limited supply of time, energy and resources available to us each day. Often we meet pressing or urgent needs and postpone or neglect more important ones. We become so busy that we have no time to sharpen the saw or to maintain the vision which the gifts of Understanding, Wisdom and Knowledge open up before us.

The gift of Fear

The fear of the Lord the Bible speaks of is not a servile fear but a healthy response to the danger of neglecting what is truly important. Fear invites us to take responsibility for the pearl of great price or the gift the Father, Jesus and the Spirit offer us in revealing themselves completely to us. (Mt 13:44-45) Fear, as the Bible understands it, approaches God's love for us with a wise head as well as with a joyful heart. 'The fear of the Lord is glory and exultation, and gladness and a crown of rejoicing ... To fear the Lord is fullness of wisdom; she inebriates mortals with her fruits; The fear of the Lord is the crown of wisdom, making peace and perfect health to flourish.' (Sir 1:11-20)

A Vital Decision

A young man was walking along a road one day when he met someone carrying two bundles, one large and the other small. On being offered a choice between the two the young man decided to go and consult the elders before making a decision. While he was away some other people came along the road and they were given the same choice. They were curious to know what each of the bundles contained and were told that the small one contained life and the other contained many of the good things of life. They asked to see the contents of the large bundle and immediately on seeing these they chose them. Ever since it has been difficult for people to choose life.

We are all called to choose between two ways, one leading to life and the other to death. 'I call heaven and earth to witness against you today that I have set before you life and death, blessings and curses. Choose life so that you and your descendants may live.' (Deut 30:15-20, Ps 1)

Two roads diverged in a wood, and I –
I took the one less travelled by,
And that has made all the difference.
(Robert Frost)

Fear and the pedagogy of responsibility

In his book, *The Seven Gifts of the Holy Spirit*, Cardinal Martini, commenting on the gift of Fear, says that Jesus does not use a pedagogy of fear in the gospels but one of responsibility. If we do not distinguish between the two we may, in a world in which fear is pervasive, interpret many of Jesus' statements in terms of a pedagogy of fear. Even though we profess belief in a God who loves us personally, the mention of 'fear of the Lord' can easily cause us to revert to an image of a God who primarily rewards and punishes. What Jesus wants us to be fearful of is the danger of not taking responsibility for our freedom. Because of the three essential temptations, to pleasure, power and sloth, we tend to choose other ways than the way which leads to life. In one of his most challenging parables Jesus depicts the tragedy of not taking responsibility for choosing the way that leads to life. 'Enter through the narrow gate; for the gate is wide and the road is easy that leads to destruction, and there are many who take it. For the gate is narrow and the road is hard that leads to life, and there are few who find it.' (Mt 7:13-14)

Taking responsibility for the gift of God

Jesus often returns to this theme of 'life' as it is essentially what he has come to give us in all its abundance. (Jn 10:10) For him, life consists in our coming to know that we are loved by God in the concrete way Jesus personifies this love in each gospel story. (Jn 17:3) It is this love the Spirit opens us up to through the gifts of Understanding, Wisdom and Knowledge. There are two fundamental ways we experience this love: as immanent, close to us and deeply involved in our life and as transcendent, distant, mysterious and overwhelming. The gift of Fear strikes a healthy balance between the two.

We have an example of the two in Moses' experience of the burning bush. He was fascinated by and wanted to draw near to it and at the same time he was overcome with reverence and a sense of deep obeisance and surrender. He took off his shoes and 'hid his face, for he was afraid to look at God'. (Ex 3:1-6) Later on in his story we see how he surrendered his whole self to walk in God's ways: '... fear the Lord your God all the days of your life, and keep all his decrees and his commandments ... You shall love the Lord your God with all your heart, and with all your soul, and with all your might'. (Deut 6:2, 5) At the heart of God's commandments is the Great Commandment that invites us primarily to be loved with our whole being and then to love God in return with every ounce of energy his love gives to us.

Love is Lord of all

The Spirit's gift of Fear heightens our awareness of how appropriate the responses of awe, reverence and surrender are to the overwhelming nature of God's love. It is our fascination with God's love and its glory that sets us free to worship and surrender with our whole heart. The source of this fascination is the awesome splendour of God's love revealed in the face of Jesus.

We catch a glimpse of this in the Transfiguration when Jesus gives his disciples a preview of himself as their risen Lord. They are enraptured with his glory and at the same time over-whelmed and even terrified by it. Peter, years later, remembered that experience of 'seeing his majesty with his own eyes'. (Mt 17:1-8, 2 Pet 1:16-18, 2 Cor 4:6) It was through their experience of Jesus' love and its glory that he became for them 'the Lord'; the one due their ultimate reverence and obedience.

In *The Principle and Foundation of the Spiritual Exercises*, Saint Ignatius of Loyola puts before us an attitude to God that the Spirit's gift of Fear makes us sensitive and responsive to. It states that we are made to know God intimately and, in response, to praise, reverence and serve him. (Eph 1:1-14, 3:14-21) Everything is given to us to attain this end. (Phil 3:8) Therefore, we must use what helps us and let go of what hampers our attaining this 'one thing necessary'. (Lk 10:38-42) We must seek freedom from the dominance of anything other than God. (Rom 6:16) Thus we become free to choose the best way to enter the intimate relation-ship that God's love and its glory opens up for us. (Jn 17:3)

> God looks on nature with a glorious eye
> And blesses all creation with the sun
> Its drapery of green and brown, earth, ocean, he
> In morning of creation just begun
> The saffron East foretells the rising sun
> And who can look upon that majesty
> Of light brightness and splendour not feel won
> With love of him whose bright all-seeing eye
> Feeds the day's light with Immortality?
> *(John Clare)*

AN EXERCISE: Make a list of the important things and then of the urgent things you give your attention to in a normal day. Next, reflect on what was on your mind yesterday and notice whether you were more engaged by urgent than by important things. Then, reflect on the story about taking time to sharpen the saw and finally reflect on Mt 13:44-45.

The Gift of Piety

The film *Lantana* is the story of four couples whose relationships are intertwined like the branches of a shrub called Lantana. Our attention is focused particularly on the relationship between Leon and his wife Sonja. He is having an affair and this is damaging his relationship with his wife and their two sons. A crisis occurs when Sonja's counsellor is killed and Leon, being the detective in charge of the murder investigation, comes across the tapes of Sonja's counselling sessions. On one of these tapes she is asked whether she still loves her husband and she says she does. On hearing the way she says this, Leon breaks into uncontrollable sobbing and shortly after returns home to ask Sonja's forgiveness. Even though what he has done has caused her terrible pain she agrees to stay in the relationship. The closing scene presents them dancing together and while it is obvious she is still recovering from the wounds he has inflicted on her, his gaze is totally fixed on her.

When Jesus was asked about the meaning of life he said if we want to have life to the full we must engage our whole person, body and soul, mind and heart, in the love we receive and return within our relationships. (Lk 10:25-28) Like Leon, we tend not to commit our whole person to our relationships because doing so is onerous. But we also find an echo in ourselves of Sonja's desire to commit her whole self to her marriage. She tells her therapist she wants her marriage to be 'passionate, challenging and emotionally honest'. Getting involved in this way in our relationships with God, ourselves and others is what the Spirit's gift of Piety is all about.

Whereas Fear enables us to face the awesomeness of the extent and depth of God's love, Piety enables us to 'abide in' it.

'As the Father has loved me, so I have loved you; abide in my love. If you keep my commandments, you will abide in my love, just as I have kept my Father's commandments and abide in his love.' (Jn 15:9-10) When Jesus invites us to 'abide in' his love and says this involves keeping his commandments, he means he wants us to involve our whole person, 'heart, soul, mind and strength' in our relationship with him.

Relating with your whole soul

To abide in Jesus' love we are invited to get our 'whole soul' or the intuitive side of ourselves engaged in listening to his self-revelation as love. The Spirit leads us into this revelation, expressed by Jesus in the gospel stories and in the Mass. 'When the Spirit of truth comes, he will guide you into all the truth.' (Jn 16:13) For example, as we listen to a gospel story or reflect on the love of someone we know, the Spirit with the gift of Piety urges us to notice and listen to the love Jesus invites us to believe in.

Relating with your whole heart

After listening to the love the Spirit brings to our attention, Piety invites us to respond with our 'whole heart' or by saying how we feel about what we have listened to. Being emotionally honest in this way about what is said to us makes a major contribution to our relationships. Therefore, after we have listened to what God says to us, the Spirit urges us to respond by saying how we feel about this, for example, in a prayer of praise and thanksgiving: '... be filled with the Spirit, as you sing psalms and hymns and spiritual songs among yourselves, singing and making melody to the Lord in your hearts, giving thanks to God the Father at all times and for everything in the name of our Lord Jesus Christ.' (Eph 5:17-20)

> *Winter Magic*
> A crumb of bread,
> For such expenditure I've been repaid
> With three clear silvery notes,
> Three lingering notes,
> Thrilled from the little throat
> Of one small bird,

And all the frost-bound earth
Burst forth
In flowers of Spring,
And bridal dresses robed the trees
Tissued with sprays of blush-white blossom,
And the air was heavy
With the fresh earth's smell
And drowsy with the hum of honey bees –
Such magic lies in three clear rippling notes
Trilled by a little bird
In thanksgiving
For one small crumb of bread.
(Anonymous)

Relating with your whole mind
If we continue to listen and respond to what God says to us we will get our 'whole mind' involved in assimilating what he reveals to us and develop the convictions that constitute our faith. There are two ways of developing these convictions, an active and a passive way. The active way is through prayer by which we change our minds and hearts as we listen and respond to the good news. (Mk 1:14-15) The passive way goes largely unnoticed as it is brought about by life's hard grind, by its hardships, its darkness and its suffering. These can make us bitter or better according as we see them in the context of God's providence or not. We have an example of this in the way Jesus led two of his disciples to see their sufferings in the context of God's word and the Mass. (Lk 24:13-35)

> I feel myself more than ever in the hands of God. It is what I have desired all my life, since I was young. And it is also the one thing that I still want now. But with one difference: today all the initiative is in the hands of the Lord. I assure you that to know myself and to feel myself totally in his hands is a profound experience. *(Pedro Arrupe)*

Relating with your whole strength
Finally, Piety urges us to get our 'whole strength' or our body with all its senses, involved in the way we relate. We do this by acting justly and living consistently with what we believe. 'If we live by the Spirit, let us also be guided by the Spirit.' (Gal 5:25) In

practice, our conscience will urge us to live consistently with what we believe. For example, it will urge us to discern how we treat others if we are to live consistently with our vision of each person as the temple of the Spirit.

We have seen how the Spirit's gift of Piety enables us to listen and respond to God's self-revelation and thereby to grow in our faith in this vision of love. We have seen too how Piety urges us to act justly or in a way that is consistent with this vision. However, the laws devised to act justly easily lose their meaning and importance when the vision they have their roots in is not maintained. The effect of this can be that people either disregard their religion because they identify it with meaningless laws or they make a religion out of these laws. 'Well then, does God supply you with the Spirit and work miracles among you by your doing the works of the law, or by your believing what you heard?' (Gal 3:5) In the light of all of this, Piety assumes its proper role when it maintains the vision that we are in the hands of a loving and provident God and when it urges us to live out of this vision by acting justly, loving tenderly and walking humbly before our God. (Mic 6:8)

> I said to the man who stood at the gate of the year,
> 'Give me a light that I may tread safely into the unknown.'
> And he replied, 'Go out into the darkness
> and put your hand into the hand of God.
> That shall be to you better than light
> and safer than a known way!'
> So I went forth and finding the Hand of God,
> trod gladly into the night.
> (M. Louise Haskins)

AN EXERCISE: Read Lk 10:25-28 and Jn 15:9-11 and notice what Jesus asks you to do if you want to have a full and happy life. Then, let Jesus join you and listen to how he affirms you for the way you receive and return his love with your whole heart, soul, mind and strength. Finally, let him ask you what way you want to relate with him in future.

The Gift of Fortitude

The film *Good Will Hunting* tells the story of a young man called Will who is sentenced to do community service as a janitor in a prestigious university. One day when he is cleaning a lecture room he sees a complicated mathematical problem written on a blackboard. He studies it and then writes the solution. When it is discovered that he is the one who has done this, the lecturer who set the problem wants to get him to exploit his talent. However, another lecturer, who is counselling Will, wants him to solve the problem which is preventing him from taking responsibility for his life. It gradually emerges that Will is not able to get involved in relationships because of fears and guilt from his past. He is also dominated by his anger which prevents him from moving ahead with his life. After Will is released from his demons he is free to set off on a journey in search of the girl who had loved him but whom he had been unable to respond to at an earlier time.

Like Will we all carry wounds from our past and need a lot of courage to take the necessary steps to heal them. Most of these wounds spring from events in which we have felt diminished and these events have contributed to the most basic wound of all which is a sense of our insignificance. We also need courage to do what is required to free ourselves from the demons that hold us captive. These demons often take the form of negative feelings like fear or anger that dominate us. The prevalence and the seriousness of the wounds life inflicts on us and of the way our demons enslave us led Jesus to spend so much of his time healing people and freeing them from their demons. In fact, Luke sets Jesus' life within a framework of healing, casting out demons and proclaiming the good news. 'The Spirit of the Lord is upon me, because he has anointed me to bring good news to the poor. He has sent me to proclaim release to the captives and recovery of sight to the blind, to let the oppressed go free.' (Lk 4:18) It is faith in this good news that Jesus proclaims which heals us and sets us free. (Lk 7:50, 18:42)

The courage that Piety calls for

Answering Jesus' essential call to faith and to the repentance it requires involves undertaking a difficult journey. This can be compared to the Exodus journey in which Moses led the people out of Egypt and then for forty years across the desert till they reached the Promised Land. Just as the people in the Exodus were called to leave the land where they were slaves, we too are called to leave our distorted ways of seeing God so that we might reach the Promised Land that faith in the good news of God's love and providence opens up before us. This is a long and demanding journey on which we must face all the hardships involved in the constant effort to repent and believe the good news. Even though Christians have found the most effective way of doing this is through prayer, they have found it very difficult to persevere in it. Is this the reason why Jesus, when he talks about prayer, mentions perseverance or 'endurance' in the same breath? 'But as for that in the good soil, these are the ones who, when they hear the word, hold it fast in an honest and good heart, and bear fruit with patient endurance.' (Lk 8:15)

> When one brings together all of Jesus' teachings on prayer, one finds that they contain practically only one recommendation: perseverance. He repeats and repeats, and keeps coming back to the subject with different parables, all bearing on the same theme, so much so that the discovery is almost disappointing. *(Rene Voillaume)*

In this context we can understand the nature of the Spirit's gift of Fortitude as what gives us the courage to answer the essential call of the Christian life. This is to make space in our lives to listen and respond to God's self-revelation and to take responsibility for the change of mind and heart that faith in this revelation calls for. (Mk 1:14-15) Hope is the virtue most closely allied to the gift of Fortitude. Hope urges us to undertake the journey in search of faith while the gift of Fortitude gives us the courage to face the difficulties essential to this journey. The greatest difficulty we face is that of the disciplined effort involved in following the way the Spirit leads us into 'all the truth'. (Jn 16:13)

Christian combat

A symbol of the struggle for which the Christian needs this gift of Fortitude is given in the book of Genesis where Jacob wrestles with God. This is necessary if he is satisfy his deepest longing, to know God 'face to face'. 'You shall no longer be called Jacob, but Israel, (The one who strives with God) for you have striven with God and with humans, and have prevailed.' Then Jacob asked him, 'Please tell me your name.' But he said, 'Why is it that you ask my name?' And there he blessed him. So Jacob called the place Peniel, saying, 'For I have seen God face to face, and yet my life is preserved.' (Gen 32:24-32) In our struggle to know God face to face through perseverance in prayer we need to 'put on the whole armour of God' (Eph 6:10-20)

> I want to know if you have
> touched the centre of your sorrow, if you have been
> opened up by life's betrayals or have
> become shrivelled and closed from fear of further pain.
> I want to know if you can sit with pain,
> mine or your own.
> *(Oriah Mountain Dreamer, A Native American Elder)*

Confirmation and confessing our faith

As well as our inner struggle to know God we have to contend with indifference or opposition to our faith from the outside. In his book on the seven gifts of the Holy Spirit, Cardinal Martini writes: 'Fortitude is the gift which gives us the capacity to confess our faith even amidst contradictions and dangers.' For Jesus, this opposition is as much a part of our lives as it was of his. 'When they hand you over, do not worry about how you are to speak or what you are to say; for what you are to say will be given to you at that time; for it is not you who speak, but the Spirit of your Father speaking through you ... you will be hated by all because of my name. But the one who endures to the end will be saved. (Mt 10:19-22)

Fortitude is part of the 'power' we receive as Christians, and especially in the sacrament of Confirmation, to be witnesses to Jesus. 'But you will receive power when the Holy Spirit comes upon you, and you will be my witnesses in Jerusalem, throughout Judea and Samaria, and to the ends of the earth.' (Acts 1:8) In the Acts of the Apostles we see how the gift of Fortitude makes the apostles, who were so fearful before Pentecost, absolutely fearless: 'And we are witnesses to these things, and so is the Holy Spirit whom God has given to those who obey him.' (Acts 5:32) All through the Acts the disciples seem to thrive on adversity; it seems that, 'Storms make oaks take deeper root.' (George Herbert)

'You will be my witnesses'

How central Fortitude is to the gospels can be seen from the following words of Jesus: 'If the world hates you, be aware that it hated me before it hated you. If you belonged to the world, the world would love you as its own. Because you do not belong to the world, but I have chosen you out of the world – therefore the world hates you. (Jn 15:18-27) It is significant that Jesus said these words in chapters 14-17 of John's gospel indicating that our sufferings are an integral part of his sublime plan for us.

> Sweet are the uses of adversity;
> Which like the toad, ugly and venomous,
> Wears yet a precious jewel in his head;
> And this our life, exempt from public haunt
> Finds tongues in trees, books in running brooks,
> sermons in stones and good in everything.
> *(William Shakespeare)*

AN EXERCISE: Describe an event in your story when you felt what you valued most was under threat from forces inside yourself. What form of indifference, hostility, hardship, darkness or suffering caused by forces outside yourself do you feel most threatened by? Read either Rom 5:1-5, Jn 16:13-15 or Mt 10:19-22 with a view to talking to the Spirit about the role her gift of Fortitude plays in your life.

The Gift of Counsel

Finding the Lion in the Stone

When the little boy asked the sculptor how he knew the magnificent lion he had carved was in the stone, he eventually got the answer, 'I had to find the lion in my heart before I could find it in the stone!' Even though the sculptor had to find it in his heart first he would not have been happy just to leave it there. It had to be given concrete expression and that had to be in harmony with what was in his heart. Giving it concrete expression is no easy task for the sculptor must wrestle with the stone until what he chisels out of it is in keeping with what he has found in his heart.

So far we have seen how, with the help of the gifts of the Spirit, we can find the lion in our hearts. It now remains for us to find the lion in the stone or to make sure that the way we live is in keeping with the vision we have found in our hearts. To live consistently with this vision involves learning the art of loving and it is this that the gift of Counsel facilitates. Where Piety, with the help of conscience, helps us to judge what is fair, just, or right in the way we act, Counsel, with the 'supernatural tact' it gives, judges what is 'just right' or in harmony with the vision which faith gives us. This heightened sensitivity is like that of artists who know when their work of art is just right or as good as they can get it. Mary Sardon in her *Journal of a Solitude* writes of the artfulness of a person who came to help her with her housework.

> When she leaves, the house is at peace. Beauty and order have returned, and always she has left behind a drop of balm; so her work here is a work of art. There is a mystical rite under that material act of cleaning and tidying for

what is done with love is always more than itself and partakes of the celestial orders.

Counsel and Jesus' commandment

The importance of Counsel springs from its relationship with Jesus' commandment that we love others as he has loved us. (Jn 15:12) The emphasis in this commandment is more on vision than on behaviour because the way we treat others is influenced mainly by the way we see them. Our vision of others is determined by the way we see and feel about ourselves, and this is determined by who we believe we are in Jesus' eyes. In other words, in the Christian's eyes every person must be seen and treated as the one for whom Christ died and it is the role of the Spirit's gift of Counsel to discern the right way to treat a person of such dignity. 'This is my commandment, that you love one another as I have loved you. No one has greater love than this, to lay down one's life for one's friends.' (Jn 15:12-13)

Counsel's heightened consciousness

Through the gift of Counsel, the Spirit gives us an instinct for what is harmonious, radiant and beautiful about the way to relate. As a result, our way of relating with others reflects back to those we love a sense of their own beauty or glory and invites them to believe in what we are saying to them by our words and gestures. What before may have been done out of duty is now, with the help of Counsel, done out of joy because of the ease that this gift brings to the way we relate.

> *Duty and joy*
> I slept and dreamt
> That life was joy –
> I awoke and found
> That life was duty –
> I acted and behold
> Duty was joy.
> *(Tagore)*

The Grace of God is in Courtesy

If Counsel develops our capacity to love others as Jesus has loved us, this gift has a special interest in coming to know the great skill with which Jesus loves and relates with us. Because of the difficulty of developing and changing the images we have of Jesus, we tend to live with a very limited range of these. This is largely because we do not take the pains to notice and put words on how the Spirit enlightens us about the many forms Jesus' love takes and the attractiveness of each of these. If we do attend to the way the Spirit leads us into Jesus' love and its attractiveness, our instinct for what is the loving thing to do becomes clearer, surer and more decisive. (Jn16:13) In the Acts of the Apostles we often find statements like the following about how clear and sure people were of what the Spirit was guiding them towards: 'The Spirit told me to go with them and not to make a distinction between them and us.' (Acts 11:12) This refined sense that Counsel gives us of how to love others in a God-like way, led the poet Hilaire Belloc to find in Courtesy 'the Grace of God.'

> Of Courtesy it is much less
> Than Courage of heart and Holiness:
> Yet in my walks it seems to me
> That the Grace of God is in Courtesy.

The greatest and most neglected art
The gift of Counsel raises the way we relate to an art form, to the art of loving. Though this is the supreme art it is also, as Erich Fromm remarks in his book, *The Art of Loving*, the most neglected one. The reason why we neglect it may be that we do not recognise its beauty or that we do not see that the most profound beauty is found in the most ordinary relationships. For example, in the film, *Three Colours: Red*, we see the charm or unostentatious splendour of Valentine's kindness in the way she relates with Joseph, an elderly judge and how the radiance of this wins him over and transforms his whole way of relating. We see the same splendour, or what the Bible calls glory, in the unobtrusive kindness of Jesus at the wedding feast of Cana. 'Jesus did this, the first of his signs, in Cana of Galilee, and revealed his glory; and his disciples believed in him.' (Jn 2:11)

The environment Counsel creates
In fostering the art of loving, Counsel has a profound effect on the environment we are responsible for creating and maintain-

ing for ourselves and others. With its sensitivity to what is the most loving thing to do Counsel helps us to create an environment permeated by what Paul calls 'the fruit of the Spirit'. This is the way that the many aspects of the Spirit's love unfold in a person's life as he or she matures. These aspects of love are often revealed in the way mature people relate with such effortless skill that we hardly notice how well they relate. Paul lists the following as the fruit of the Spirit: 'joy, peace, patience, kindness, goodness, faithfulness, gentleness and self-control'. (Gal 5:22-23) There are other aspects of the love the Spirit gives us a gift of, such as those listed in 1 Cor 13:4-7, that build up the Christian community as the caring environment or fellowship in which the Spirit wants us to live.

When Yeats wrote his poem, *A Prayer for my Daughter*, he was conscious of how the pursuit of outer beauty can send the inner kind to sleep. It is this inner beauty, found in the different aspects of love we call 'the fruit of the Spirit', that Counsel wants to awaken us to, so that we might pursue it.

> May she be granted beauty and yet not
> Beauty to make a stranger's eye distraught,
> or hers before a looking glass, for such
> Being made beautiful overmuch,
> Consider beauty a sufficient end,
> Lose natural kindness and maybe
> The heart-revealing intimacy
> That chooses right, and never find a friend.

AN EXERCISE: In the quiet of your inner room be in the presence of some of the significant people in your life. These may be your mother or father, your husband or wife, a close friend, a member of your family or someone with whom you work. Ask each of the people present to comment on your style of loving and write down the most moving thing that each of them says to you. After the others have left, enter into a dialogue with the person whose estimation of you moved you most.

PART 5

Introduction

In Part 5 we look at the path along which the Spirit leads us into the love of God. There are three ages in the growth of this love: affection, passionate love and friendship. Affection involves four loves: acceptance; appreciation; concern and personal love. Passionate love builds on the foundation laid by these loves and has the dramatic effect of taking us out of preoccupation with self to centre our affection on another person. When passionate love becomes permanent and profound it finds fulfilment in friendship and in the joyful love that is at friendship's core.

The chapters in Part 5 deal firstly with *Eros*, the basic natural love at the source of our dream. Because of its human limitations Eros needs the unlimited love of *Agape* or Jesus' love of us to the 'utmost extent' if it is to realise its dream. The gateway to the love the Spirit wants to lead us into is *Acceptance*. If we do not accept our limitations and sinfulness we will not be able to *Appreciate* all the goodness and beauty God finds in us. Besides teaching us to appreciate all that is, the Spirit teaches us a *Provident love* or a concern for all of our dream yet to be realised. This acceptance, appreciation and concern leads to a sense of significance, or a *Personal love* we experience when we meet Jesus face to face in a gospel story or at Mass. In coming to know Jesus and the attractiveness of his love we experience a love more *Passionate* than any human falling in love. This Passionate love gives us the power to change our minds and hearts and to believe that we are loved enduringly and deeply. This experience of a love that is *Permanent* and *Profound* opens the way to the love that Jesus calls *Friendship*. This consists in sharing in the divine life of the Father, Jesus and the Spirit, sharing in their love, their glory and their union which is pervaded by their *Joyful love*.

Three ages of love and relationship

The age of affection: as children we receive:

> A love that accepts us
>
> A love that appreciates and delights in us
>
> A provident love that cares for us
>
> A personal love that finds us uniquely significant

The age of passionate love: loving another as Jesus has loved us

> We want for another the dream we want for ourselves,
>
> the dream Jesus passionately wants us to realise,
>
> of a love whose beauty draws us into union and its joy

The age of friendship: when passionate love becomes:

> Permanent: we want our love and its dream to last
>
> Profound: we want our love to deepen
>
> so that it finds fulfilment in friendship
>
> and in the joyful love at friendship's core

CHAPTER 30

Eros

In this chapter we will examine Eros as the dream, the design or the plan, and the energy to realise it, that God builds into everything. The pervasiveness of Eros is thus described by St Augustine:

> When all is said and done, is there any more marvellous sight, any occasion when human reason is nearer some form of communication with the nature of things, than the sowing of seeds, the planting of cuttings, the transplanting of shrubs, the grafting of slips? It is as though you could question the vital force in each root and bud on what it can do, and what it cannot, and on the source of its ability and inability, (or to question it) on what is due to its own internal power of growth and what to the care that is given it from without; and thinking about that, remember that neither the one who plants nor the one who waters is anything, but only God who gives the growth; (1 Cor 3:7) because whatever in the work is added from without, is added by someone whom God created, governs and invisibly directs.

In human beings Eros has its roots in the image of God we are created in and that makes us capable of a God-like love. As a result, love is not just what we desire or long for but what we *are* a hunger for. This hunger emerges in life as our dream of a love for which God has made us; a dream too of the intimacy and the joy that the innate attractiveness of this love draws us into.

> As the tree's sap doth seek the root below
> In winter, in my winter now I go
> Where none but thee, the eternal root
> Of true love, I may know. (*John Donne*)

The love we call Eros and the intimacy and joy it draws us into is so attractive or beautiful it engages our whole person. We see this when we fall in love, how it engages us at the four levels at which we relate. For example, there is a movement of our senses and intuitive powers to become aware of the signs of love we receive and a movement of our heart and mind towards making our own of this love so that it becomes a conviction that we are loved. This conviction is prized for it is the source of our life and happiness. 'The supreme happiness in life is the conviction that we are loved.' (Victor Hugo)

Eros as delight as well as desire

An important aspect of Eros is that it is a mixture of desire and delight, of longing for what might be and of enjoyment of what is. Even though Eros is primarily delight it is seen in our time almost exclusively as desire. Thus, we devote most of our energies to our concern for all that yet might be rather than celebrating the areas of our dream that are already realised. Even though Eros is primarily delight and we have a natural preference for a culture of enjoyment, there is something unrealistic to our ears about the saying 'Every creature, with the exception of man, knows that the main business of life is to enjoy it.'

> Joy (my wife) tells me that once, years ago, she was haunted one morning by a feeling that God wanted something of her, a persistent pressure like the nag of a neglected duty. And till mid-morning she kept on wondering what it was. But the moment she stopped worrying, the answer came through as plain as a spoken word. It was: 'I don't want you to do anything, I want to give you something' and immediately her heart was peace and delight.
> (C. S. Lewis)

A preference for affirmation

Since Eros is more an experience of delight than of desire it favours affirmation more than correction as a means of fostering growth. Affirmation here is taken to mean mainly an appreciation of all that we already are though it also includes a concern for all we yet may be. However, if we are to affirm others in the way Eros urges us to, we must first of all accept their limitations and weaknesses or these will generate negative feelings that make it difficult for us to affirm them. From acceptance and affirmation comes a sense of worth, dignity and glory that people see in each other's eyes and ask each other to believe in. Thus, the affirmation Eros engenders is built on the foundation of acceptance and finds fulfilment in a sense of personal significance.

Eros as catalyst

A sense of being accepted and affirmed creates a 'holding environment' where we feel significant and secure. When we are children this environment is created by our parents' acceptance and affirmation of us. However, as adults we take responsibility for cultivating this environment for ourselves as well as for others. This transition from infancy and adolescence, when our world centres on meeting our own needs, to adulthood, when we are asked to love others as we do ourselves, is a very difficult one. For this Exodus in each person's life we need the catalyst that Eros' passionate love supplies when, for example, we fall in love. This experience of Eros has the power to move us out of our self-preoccupation so that we gradually become capable of centring our whole person on another.

Can the dream last?

The fragility of human love and the rocky periods all relationships go through ask us questions like: Can the dream of love with all its attractiveness and the intimacy and joy it draws us into be made to last? Can the dream of passionate love deepen so that it finds fulfilment in friendship and joy? A fuller answer to these questions is to be found in the remaining chapters of this book. For now, we will outline how Eros urges us to pursue our dream of a love that gradually becomes permanent and profound and thus finds fulfilment in friendship.

For the love called Eros to become more permanent we must learn to accept our limitations and for it to become more profound we must learn to appreciate our gifts. Becoming aware of and taking responsibility for coming to know these two sides of ourselves in this way means that we have a self to share; we become capable of real intimacy, defined as making known our inmost self, and thus of friendship.

The tragedy of not attending to our relationships and to the way Eros would have them grow is that no amount of material things will fill the hole left by the absence of the joy which the development of these relationships were designed to bring.

> Countries like ours are full of people who have all the material comforts they desire, yet lead lives of quiet (and at times noisy) desperation, understanding nothing but the fact that there is a hole inside them and that however much food and drink they pour into it, however many motorcars and television sets they stuff it with, however many well-balanced children and loyal friends they parade around the edges of it ... it aches! *(Bernard Levin)*

> Striving too hard begets a troubled mind
> And those who strive will always stay confined.
> For you are not the body, not the mind
> But LIGHT IMMORTAL, mortally enshrined.
> *(Robert Goslin)*

EXERCISE: Tell the story of a time in your life when your dream of love, intimacy and joy surfaced for you. Write down some ways your dream is already realised. Take time to delight in and be grateful for this. What are the areas of your dream you are hopeful that you can still realise? Enter a dialogue with Eros and the dream it is always urging you to realise. After you have both said all you want to say, spend time reflecting on how you see and feel about each other.

Agape

Bread and Cheese or a Banquet

A family from Eastern Europe decided to emigrate to the United States. They sold their home and land and only had enough money to pay their fare. Their neighbours were poor people but they gave them lots of bread and cheese for the journey. On the second week when they were well out to sea one of the children could no longer take any more bread and cheese so his father gave him a little money to buy an apple. When the child did not come back the father went searching for him and found him in the dining hall surrounded by all kinds of food. When he complained to his son that they could never afford this meal he was told that the whole family could have had it every day as it was included in the price of their ticket.

Agape is the banquet or superabundance of love that Eros intimates and even promises but cannot provide on its own. By itself Eros cannot overcome our human limitations and sinfulness and fulfil our dream. If we do not face this fact and if we strive to fulfil our dream, using our human resources in an attempt to meet needs that only God can meet, we will not enter the banquet God invites us to but live on bread and cheese.

> Western culture is marked by the fatal attempt to secure the good of humanity by eliminating God. *(John Paul II)*

Without God we are limited and cannot satisfy the hunger we are for a love that is not limited. As a result, the lack of love or of acceptance and affirmation that people experience in their human relationships leaves them with a deeply ingrained sense of insignificance, a sense that their lives do not amount to much. This is the essential human pain and to escape it we try to make ourselves significant by devoting our energies to earning it.

However, the work we do and the wealth we acquire cannot supply the love that would alleviate our pain and so we experience a sense of anxiety, frustration and sadness.

Our need of a catalyst
We are in need of a catalyst, a person whose love is strong enough to change our mind and heart so that we believe beyond all doubt that we are loved, that we are profoundly significant. Jesus is such a catalyst in the passionate love he expresses for us in his life, death and resurrection. In his death especially we experience his love of us to the utmost extent, the greatest love the world has ever known. (Jn 13:1, 15:13) 'By the cross we know the gravity of sin and the greatness of God's love towards us.' (John Chrysostom) In the remaining chapters of this book we will explore the extent and depth of this love. That we do so is vital if Jesus' love is to retain its power as a catalyst to bring about the change of mind and heart that belief in this love calls for. This belief opens to us 'God's eternal bounty' when God 'spends himself in giving us himself, his treasure, in making man a God omnipotent'. (2 Pet 1:4)

> *Incarnatio est maximum Dei donum*
> So God's eternal bounty ever shined
> The beams of being, moving, life, sense, mind,
> And to all things himself communicated.
> But see the violent diffusive pleasure
> Of goodness, that left not till God had spent
> Himself by giving us himself, his treasure,
> In making man a God omnipotent.
> How might this goodness draw our souls above,
> Which drew down God with such attractive love.
> *(William Alabaster)*

The passion with which Jesus loves us
In the Great Commandment Jesus invites us to respond to his passionate love in a passionate way, to receive and return this love with our 'whole heart and soul, mind and strength'. This is what is called for as our response to the fact that Jesus loves us with all the intensity with which his Father loves him. If we discover and gradually learn to believe in the glory or intense at-

tractiveness of this love we will be drawn to immerse our whole person in it. (Jn 15:9-10)

Can passionate love last?

What often obstructs our immersing ourselves in Jesus' love is the distorted images of him we have inherited and harbour. If we have grown up with images of God as remote, detached, dispassionate and perhaps as judgemental and demanding, then the idea of him loving us with a passion may seem unrealistic and misleading. Even at a human level, in a marriage for example, it may seem unrealistic to expect love to remain passionate. We may associate this passion or intensity with falling in love and the early days of our relationship or with key moments in it. However, the rocky road we travel into our closest relationships may not lead us to expect its intensity to be an abiding experience. This leads people to be uncomfortable with talk about God's love or human love remaining passionate. How it can remain so, though in a different way than we imagine, is the point Dr Janis makes to his daughter as she decides who she will marry:

> Love is a temporary madness, it erupts like volcanoes and then subsides. And when it subsides you have to make a decision. You have to work out whether your roots have so entwined together that it is inconceivable that you should ever part. Because that is what love is. Love is not breathlessness, it is not excitement, it is not the promulgation of promises of eternal passion ... That is just being 'in love', which any fool can do. Love itself is what is left over when being in love has burned away, and this is both an art and a fortunate accident. Your mother and I had it, we had roots that grew towards each other underground, and when all the pretty blossoms had fallen from our branches we found that we were one tree and not two. But sometimes the petals fall away and the roots have not entwined. Imagine giving up your home and your people, only to discover after six months, a year, three years, that the trees had no roots and have fallen over. Imagine the desolation. Imagine the imprisonment. (*L de Bernieres, Captain Corelli's Mandolin*)

As passionate love develops it may seem to lose its intensity, because when it deepens it tends to become quieter and less obvious, moving as it does from seeing to faith. The importance of this development is highlighted by Jesus after his resurrection when Thomas cannot accept the new way Jesus is present to him and hankers after the more tangible and visible way Jesus was present prior to his resurrection. (Jn 20:24-29) When passionate love rests on our convictions of being loved more than on what is sensed, felt or glimpsed, it offers us a much more permanent kind of presence and joy. However, if it is to continue to engage us wholly and deeply we must often return to its roots. These are to be found in our experience of those who love us as well as in the sensate details of the gospel stories and the imagery, insight and feeling these stories generate. By returning to these roots, our faith in the passionate love of Jesus becomes more real, colourful, engaging and even enrapturing.

Who more can crave
Than thou hast done,
That gav'st a son
To free a slave,
First made of nought,
With all since bought?
(Ben Jonson)

AN EXERCISE: What is your view of passionate love? What images and feelings are stirred up in you when you think of human love in these terms? What images are stirred up when you think of God's or Jesus' love in this way? What way does God want you to be engaged by his love? Does he want you to understand, be involved in, engrossed with or enraptured by his love? Be before Jesus on the cross and having reflected on Jn 13:1 or Jn 15:13 speak to him about this dramatic expression of his love for you.

The love that accepts us as we are

The film *The Prince of Tides* is the story of Tom Wingo and how he came to terms with the environment in which he grew up. There was much about that environment which he loved and much also about it which he hated. He loved his family and many of the people in the small town where he grew up. He hated the endless war that went on between his mother and father and what this did to his brother and sister. Most of all he hated himself because of the memory of an absolutely degrading event that was also the source of his sister's suicidal despair.

As we enter the story Tom is trying to deal with the paralysing effects of his self-doubt. To save himself and his sister Savannah, who is in hospital after attempting suicide, he is being helped to confront his past by a psychotherapist called Susan Lowenstein. Together they unravel all he hated as well as all he loved about the surroundings in which he grew up. By the end of the story Tom has come to terms with most of the circumstances of his past. He has come to accept the limitations of his environment and to appreciate the fact that the good in it far outweighed the bad.

Each of us has, like Tom Wingo, to face these two sides of ourselves. If we don't, we will live in what John Powell calls a 10% Club. This is a place where we are only 10% alive as, quite unknowingly, we realise only a fraction of the potential or possibilities our dream urges us to realise. To live life more fully we must face two realities: our human poverty or how limited and sinful we are, and our potential or how gifted and graced we are. In this chapter we will look at how we can very profitably face our poverty and graciously accept this side of ourselves as God teaches us to do. 'The shadow side of us is 90% gold.' (Carl Jung)

At the beginning of his life, even though Buddha had an abundance of this world's goods and his parents shielded him from all unpleasantness, he was not happy. Then one day when he was travelling through his kingdom he opened the window of his carriage and saw the Four Sights. He saw people looking for food, mourning a loss, caring for the ill and facing old age. These sights had such a profound effect on him that he left his kingdom in search of enlightenment. He eventually found it under the Bo Tree where he was inspired to become a Buddha for others. Wherever we go we find statues of the Buddha and he is always smiling, as having been enlightened by the woundedness of human kind he is no longer depressed by this but at peace.

If we do not accept our poverty, it tends to generate a poor self-image that develops through a number of stages. It generally begins with a negative feeling, like anger, that colours the way we see ourselves as long as our anger lasts. If we do not deal with this feeling it becomes persistent and a poor self-image takes root in us. This limits or blocks our belief in what is positive about us; what our friends and especially what God would like us to believe in. With the poet we ask in unbelief, 'What? I the centre of thy arms' embraces?'

The Divine Lover
Me, Lord? Canst thou misspend
One word, misplace one look on me?
Call'st me thy Love, thy Friend?
Can this poor soul the object be
Of these love-glances, those life-kindling eyes?
What? I the centre of thy arms' embraces?
Of all thy labour I the prize?
Love never mocks, Truth never lies.
Oh how I quake: yet fear hope displaces:
I would, but cannot hope: such wondrous love amazes.
(Phineas Fletcher)

A poor self-image is like an open wound, painful and easily agitated. It puts us in touch with the most basic of human aches, the sense of insignificance or of not being worth much. This image of ourselves deprives us of our freedom to receive the huge amount of love available to us; it makes most expressions of love seem unreal and undeserved.

> We live in an atmosphere of shame. We are ashamed of everything that is real about us, ashamed of ourselves, of our relatives, of our incomes, of our accents, of our opinions, of our experience, just as we are ashamed of our naked skins. *(G. B. Shaw)*

Four levels of acceptance
In a number of radical ways Jesus fully accepts us and teaches us to accept ourselves. For example, he is content to be with us in the way he was with the two disciples he joined on the road to Emmaus. (Lk 24) We see how at home Jesus is with our waywardness in his parable about the weeds amid the wheat and in the way he deals with Zacchaeus. (Mt 13:24-30, Lk 19:1-10) 'We cannot change anything unless we accept it. Condemnation does not liberate, it oppresses.' (Carl Jung)

A second way Jesus accepts us is that he identifies with us in our weaknesses and temptations. 'For we do not have a high priest who is unable to sympathise with our weaknesses, but we have one who in every respect has been tested as we are, yet without sin.' (Heb 4:15)

A third way Jesus accepts us is that by highlighting all that is positive about us he puts our weakness and waywardness in perspective. We see an example of this in the way he related with the woman in Simon's house. (Lk 7:36-50) He teaches us to keep our eye on the doughnut and not upon the hole by highlighting the glory he shares with us. (Jn 17:22)

> We ought not to dwell upon one another's vices, but rather contemplate in each other the image of God, which by his excellence and dignity can and should move us to love them and forget all their vices which might turn us away from them. *(John Calvin)*

Another way Jesus teaches us to accept ourselves as he does is as mysterious as it is beautiful. We have an example of this in the parable of the lost sheep which symbolises how Jesus rejoices when he brings back to us our dark companion whom we are ashamed of and have banished from our sight. (Lk 15:3-7) This weak and wayward self is often the part of us that is most heroic as it is where we struggle with our limitations and temptations. Jesus sees this side of us more as a cause for celebration than shame. 'Jesus came not just to save us from our sins but to convince us that we are beautiful.' (John Chrysostom)

In Hosea 2, Ezekiel 16 and Lk 15:11-32 we see how God accepts our weakness and waywardness and even makes a feature of these in the tapestry he weaves out of all life's experiences.

The Master Craftsman

The tapestry maker weaves his artwork on a piece of gauze stretched across the centre of a room. He is on one side of this while on the other are a number of assistants each with his own colour of thread from which the tapestry is woven. The tapestry maker indicates where he requires a particular colour he wants to be pushed through the gauze and the person with that colour follows his instruction. But from time to time one of the assistants loses concentration and pushes through the wrong colour or not at the place indicated. Rather than blaming the assistant for his mistake the master craftsman, being so skilled, can incorporate it into his plan and even make it a feature of the tapestry.

AN EXERCISE: Enter your inner room and after quietening yourself notice how all the objects in your room reflect the different facets of your life. Let Jesus join you as you look at the tapestry stretching from the ceiling to the floor at the centre of your room. He speaks to you about how beautiful this tapestry of your life is. You ask him why your limitations and sinfulness do not seem to be represented and he tells you how he is the master craftsman who can weave the good and bad things of your life into this beautiful tapestry.

The love that appreciates and delights in us

In the film *Three Colours: Blue* Julie has always lived in the shadow of her husband who was a famous composer. When he and their only child are killed in a car accident she seeks solitude to mourn her loss. Rather than succumbing to the pain of it she finds a new life in her friends' concern for her and in her own new found concern for a number of people she goes out to in their need. She finds what Wordsworth calls the best portion of a good person's life in these 'little, nameless, unremembered acts of kindness and of love'. At the end of the film we are treated to the haunting Symphony for the European Union that had been begun by her husband and completed by Julie. With this music playing in the background portraits are displayed on the screen of the various people she has been good to and the words of Paul's hymn to love also appear on the screen and are narrated. 'Love is patient; love is kind; love is not envious or boastful or arrogant or rude. It does not insist on its own way; it is not irritable or resentful; it does not rejoice in wrongdoing, but rejoices in the truth. It bears all things, believes all things, hopes all things, endures all things. Love never ends.' (1 Cor 13:4-8)

In his book, *Cycles of Affirmation* Jack Dominion compares two ways of fostering people's growth. He says for the last thousand years people have believed that the best way to improve themselves and others is by correction. He suggests affirmation as a much more healthy alternative. Affirmation consists in appreciation of all that already is and concern for all that yet might be. A lesson one learns, particularly as a parent or teacher, is that correction which leaves little time for appreciation is deadening, whereas within a healthy environment established by affirmation correction can be life-giving.

God focuses on what is positive

We need to appreciate that a huge percentage of us is gifted and graced by God. This is often overshadowed by the limited and sinful side of us which, even though it only represents a small fraction of us, tends to capture our attention and dominate the image we have of ourselves. 'The consciousness of evil throws good things into the shade.'(Wis 16:12) In this context the following lines on humility are enlightening:

> The humility engendered by this experiential knowledge of God's goodness and love I call perfect ... But the humility arising from a realistic grasp of the human condition I call imperfect. *(The Cloud of Unknowing)*

The ways we are gifted and graced

To become more aware of and to appreciate the gifted and graced side of us we need to consider three kinds of gifts that abound in our lives. There are *natural gifts* such as eyesight, hearing and health, each of which is not just useful but wondrous. 'For it was you who formed my inward parts; you knit me together in my mother's womb. I praise you, for I am fearfully and wonderfully made.' (Ps 139:13-14) Then there are *personal gifts* such as the significant events and people unique to each person's story. 'You have seen him in the desert too: Yahweh your God continued to support you, as a man supports his son, all along the road you followed until you arrived here.' (Deut 1:31) Finally, there are *supernatural gifts* that follow from our being incorporated into Christ at baptism so that we 'share the divine nature', the inmost life of the Trinity. 'Through these, the greatest and priceless promises have been lavished on us, that through them you should share the divine nature.' (2 Pet 1:4)

> Why, he had once wondered, would a perfect God create the universe? To be generous with it, he believed now. For the pleasure of seeing pure gifts appreciated. Maybe that's what it meant to find God; to see what you have been given, to know divine generosity, to appreciate the large things and the small. *(Mary Doria Russell, Sparrow)*

'The Lord delights in you'

The love that appreciates is based on the fundamental reality that though love is desire it is primarily delight. This is the delight God takes in us, in who we are for him. 'You shall be a crown of beauty in the hand of the Lord, and a royal diadem in the hand of your God ... you shall be called My Delight Is in Her, and your land Married; for the Lord delights in you, and your land shall be married. For as a young man marries a young woman, so shall your builder marry you, and as the bridegroom rejoices over the bride, so shall your God rejoice over you'. (Is 62:2-5) 'You were adorned with gold and silver, while your clothing was of fine linen, rich fabric, and embroidered cloth. You grew exceedingly beautiful, fit to be a queen. Your fame spread among the nations on account of your beauty, for it was perfect because of my splendour that I had bestowed on you, says the Lord God.' (Ezek 16:10-14)

In his book, *Love*, the philosopher Josef Pieper, having surveyed a number of meanings of the word love, concludes, 'Love means to approve, to turn to someone and say, "It's good that you exist, it's good that you are in the world." ... But the will knows not only the act of striving for what it does not have, but also the other act of loving what it already possesses and rejoicing in that.'

The word delight is a much stronger word than appreciation. Whereas appreciation is a response to the attraction of what is good, delight is a response to the intense attractiveness of beauty or to the vision that enraptures us. Delight is immensely important for our relationships as it gives us a sense of significance or glory that is so life-giving. 'No one can live without delight and that is why a person deprived of spiritual joy goes over to material pleasures.' (Thomas Aquinas)

Why God delights in each person

The initial reason why God delights in us is that from the moment we were created in his image he 'has crowned us with glory and beauty'. (Ps 8) However, the ultimate reason is that, due to our baptism, we are now a new creation in Christ and share in his glory. 'The glory that you have given me I have given them.' (Jn 17:22) The fact that we are in Christ means that we are in the one in whom the Father delights. 'Here is my servant, whom I uphold, my chosen, in whom my soul delights.' (Is 42:1) Paul believes that we radiate beauty or glory in a much greater way than Moses did after he had spoken to God on the mountain and his face 'was alight with heavenly splendour'. (2 Cor 3:7) 'And all of us, with our unveiled faces like mirrors reflecting the glory of the Lord, are being transformed into the image that we reflect in brighter and brighter glory; this is the working of the Lord who is the Spirit.' (2 Cor 3:18)

We are asked to believe in 'the glory and beauty' with which God crowns each of us, that 'he sees and loves in us what he sees and loves in Christ', (Preface of the Mass) that 'we are God's work of art'. (Eph 2:10) To get an experience of this we might let God say some of the lines of the following poem to us.

How do I love thee? Let me count the ways,
I love thee in the depth and breadth and height
My soul can reach, when feeling out of sight
For the end of Being, and ideal grace.
I love thee to the level of everyday's
Most quiet need, by sun and candle-light.
I love thee freely, as men strive for Right,
I love thee purely as they turn from Praise.
I love thee with the passion put to use
In my old griefs, and with my childhood's faith.
I love thee with a love I seemed to lose
With my lost saints – I love thee with the breath,
Smiles, tears of all my life! – and if God choose,
I shall but love thee better after death.
(*Elizabeth B. Browning*)

AN EXERCISE: After reading what is written above about *Three Colours: Blue*, choose a number of people whom you have been good to in life. Let each of them express their appreciation and delight in the glimpse of glory or what is best about humanity that you have given them. Write down what they say to you and then let God express, in their words, his appreciation of and delight in you.

Provident Love

In the film *The Field of Dreams* a farmer walking through his maize field hears a voice which says, 'If you build it, he will come.' To answer this call he does something that others consider crazy: he turns his best field into a baseball park. In this way he is able to return to a time in his life when he used to go to baseball matches with his father. It is as if through reviving this experience he could revive his whole relationship with his father. As a young lad he was unaware of how well his father looked after him when his mother died. Now there is much about his father's provident concern for him and the caring environment that this created that he now, as a father himself, wants to rediscover and talk to his father about.

There are people and events we need to make space to return to as they put us in touch with the care that sustains us in life. It is when we realise all the provident love that a child needs if he or she is to grow, that we get our most tangible experience of this care that is the making of us. For example, at a certain stage in life we become more keenly aware of our parents' affection and of the huge influence this has had on our lives. C. S. Lewis in his *Four Loves* confirms this when he says that affection is 'responsible for nine tenths of whatever solid and durable happiness there is in our natural lives'. A major part of this affection is the concern of parents that their children would realise their dream; that they would find love, enduring relationships and joy.

The dream that inspires all living things
It is awesome to think that an oak tree is the realisation of something that was in the acorn from which it grew. We might call what was in the acorn a plan, a design or a dream. This was built into it and directed each stage of its

growth on its way to becoming a majestic oak tree. It did not grow at random, for even though it was shaped by circumstances such as storms, the main thrust of its growth came from the dream built into it. The tree's growth is always being directed by this design of God deep within it.

What it takes to realise our dream

Our lives too are directed by a dream God has built into us or by the design, plan or will of God. Our dream, however, differs from that in the acorn in that it is not automatically realised. We have both to become aware of it and to take responsibility for realising it. This dream was built into us when God made us in his image, capable of receiving and returning a God-like love. Becoming aware of this dream involves noticing the signs of love we receive and then we must take responsibility for engaging our whole person in making our own of this love. Realising our dream also involves developing the intimacy and joy that the radiance of this love draws us into.

What drowns out the voice of our dream

It is very easy for the voice of the Spirit, directing us into the love at the core of our dream, to be drowned out by lesser concerns. In his book *Seven Habits of Highly Effective People,* Stephen Covey distinguishes between what is important and what is urgent. When he asks people what would significantly improve their lives they always mention important things but in practice they remain addicted to what is urgent. He believes that truly effective people concentrate on what is important and concludes: 'Of course, parents are going to have to deal with crises and with putting out fires that are both important and urgent. But when they proactively choose to spend more time on things that are truly important but not necessarily urgent, it reduces the crises and the fires.'

God's dream for us, his plan for our peace

Our dream is not something we realise by our own efforts, it is God who inspires it and brings it to full flower. 'I planted, Apollos watered but God gave the growth.' (1 Cor 3:6) Yet, as St Augustine says, 'God who made us without our consent will not save us without our consent.' Though God has a dream for us, 'a plan for our peace', we must seek it with a passion or 'with all our heart'. 'For surely I know the plans I have for you, says the Lord, plans for your peace and not for harm, to give you a future full of hope. Then when you call upon me and come and pray to me, I will hear you. When you search for me, you will find me; if you seek me with all your heart.' (Jer 29:11-13)

The Christian dream of living life to the full

Jesus continues to work out this plan the Father has for our peace. He uses the word 'life' for this 'peace' or fulfilment he continues to work towards. 'I came that they may have life, and have it abundantly.' (Jn 10:10) Jesus describes life as an intimate knowledge of his love and through this of the Father's love. (Jn 17:3) When he is asked how we attain this life he says it is through getting wholly involved in receiving his love and in returning it within the main relationships of our lives. 'Just then a lawyer stood up to test Jesus. 'Teacher,' he said, 'what must I do to inherit eternal life?' He said to him, 'What is written in the law? What do you read there?' He answered, 'You shall love the Lord your God with all your heart, and with all your soul, and with all your strength, and with all your mind; and your neighbour as yourself.' And he said to him, 'You have given the right answer; do this, and you will live.' (Lk 10:25-28)

What gives us the incentive to get wholly engaged in loving others as we do ourselves is the intense attractiveness of the love of Jesus that emerges according as we become aware of his love and its beauty and learn to believe in it. The growing attractiveness of his love also draws us into a union with God, ourselves and others that Jesus says is 'complete', as he says is the joy that characterises this union. (Jn 17:13, 22-23) The unlimited possibilities of this dream of 'peace' and 'life' are unfolded before us in chapters 14-17 of John's gospel.

The role of hope

Pursuing this dream in a world that keeps reminding us of how unrealistic it is calls for the virtue of hope. This is a virtue that clarifies the object of the dream set before us by Jesus and his Spirit and gives us the incentive to pursue it. The object of hope's quest, of all that is yet to be realised of our dream, is symbolised in the Old Covenant by the Promised Land. This is what led the Israelites to set out on the Exodus and what helped them persevere in this journey over forty years until they reached the land flowing with milk and honey. (Deut 6:15) In the New Covenant the object of our hope is opened up before us with Jesus' invitation, 'Come and see.' What we are invited to see is a radiant vision of the full extent and depth of the Father's love that Jesus expresses in human terms. (Jn 1:39, 14:9) Thus our hope of knowing the love of Jesus and of being 'filled with all the fullness of God' has no boundaries. (Eph 3:18-19) Our hope is like a haunting tune that constantly allures us somewhere often not clearly defined.

> Hope is the thing with feathers
> that perches in the soul
> and sings the tune without the words
> and never stops at all.
> (Emily Dickenson)

Hope in its turn rests on poverty of spirit, for 'being filled with all the fullness of God' is beyond all our human resources. Poverty, as Jesus spoke about it in the Beatitudes, enables us to put our hand in the hand of God in a spirit of dependence, trust and complete surrender to the Spirit leading us into 'all the truth'. (Jn 16:13-15)

AN EXERCISE: List some of the urgent things you find yourself doing each day and then list some of the important things. Which of them do you make most space for in your day? Are there ways you find yourself making the urgent things a priority where you realise that you should give the important things this preference? List the most important things in your life and then number them in their order of importance. Which elements of the Christian dream of love, whose beauty draws us into intimacy and joy, do you identify most with?

Personal Love

The film *Il Postino* is about a young man called Mario who tires of his life as a fisherman and takes up the work of a postman. As such he delivers post to Pablo Neruda, a famous poet, and gradually becomes fascinated with his lifestyle. He envies the poet's facility with words, his intimacy with his wife and the fact that he is so respected by people. Mario on the contrary feels inarticulate, very much on his own in life and regards himself as a nobody. The film turns out to be about the ways Neruda draws the poet out of Mario and thus helps him to win over Beatrice who gives Mario's life the fundamental significance he has dreamed of.

Two basic needs

Like Mario, in his relationship with Beatrice, we all rely on personal love to satisfy two basic needs. We need first of all to be related with in a face to face way and not just as part of a crowd. We resent being treated in an impersonal way as if we were just a number; we want the unique person we are to be recognised and related with.

> That I am a man, this I share with other men. That I see and hear and that I eat and drink is what all animals likewise do. But that I am I is only mine and belongs to me and to nobody else; not to an angel nor to God – except insomuch as I am one with him. *(Meister Eckhart)*

Personal love also meets our need to have our human worth acknowledged. This need follows from the fact that we are made in the image of God and 'crowned with glory and beauty'. (Ps 8) We have an inbuilt need to have this glory recognised and respected.

Glory stands for the significance or importance of a person's life, what is acknowledged about them; a certain gravitas. Glory is like the integration of the features of a face, so that its integrity, its harmony and especially its splendour is glimpsed in the sensate. *(Balthasar)*

A developing sense of uniqueness

In their love for us our parents and family meet this twofold need when they accept and affirm us. When we go to school, those who befriend us choose us out of the crowd because of something distinctive about us. Rather than being just another pupil or a member of their class our friends call us by name or give us a nickname as an acknowledgement of our distinctiveness.

Besides being distinct from others we are unique. We see, feel and relate with others in a way that nobody before or after us has done or will do. Each person's story is a record of how he or she has developed a unique vision, value system and style of relating. The more we know our own story and are on our own 'thread' the more personal will be our relationships and the love we receive and give within them.

The Thread of Life

There is a thread that runs through our lives and it is absolutely unique to each person. It emerges from God, runs through all our days and inevitably makes its way back to him. 'Thee God I come from, to Thee go; all day long I like fountain flow from thy hand outstretched'. (G. M. Hopkins) It begins with God choosing us and calling the unique person in each of us, by name, into a deeply personal relationship with him. This thread is as unique to each of us as are our finger-prints, as the way we see a sunrise or hear another's voice. It symbolises the unique and very consistent way that God leads us into a personal relationship with him. We will be most content in life when we are in touch with this unique way God wants to be with each one of us.

The emergence of personal love in the Bible

Like Moses we are chosen out of the crowd to speak with God 'face to face, as one speaks with a friend.' (Ex 33:11) According to the Scripture scholar, van Rad, it is in the prophets we find, for the first time in the history of civilisation, that God wants to speak to each person. God's desire to reveal himself to 'the least no less than to the greatest' and to speak to each person's heart, is what characterises the New Covenant that Jeremiah was sent to predict. 'But this is the covenant that I will make with the house of Israel after those days, says the Lord: I will put my law within them, and I will write it on their hearts; and I will be their God, and they shall be my people. No longer shall they teach one another, or say to each other, "Know the Lord," for they shall all know me, from the least of them to the greatest, says the Lord.' (Jer 31:31-34)

'I call you by your name'
Within this one to one relationship God draws us into, he speaks to the unique person each of us is, he calls each of us by name. He speaks to each person in a way that captures what is distinct about each person's relationship with him. 'I will give you the treasures of darkness and riches hidden in secret places, so that you may know that it is I, the Lord, the God of Israel, who call you by your name. For the sake of my servant Jacob, and Israel my chosen, I call you by your name, I surname you, though you do not know me.' (Is 45:3-4)

> The sun shines upon a certain spot on earth and gives it no less light than if it shone nowhere else, and shone only for that place. In the very same manner our Lord thinks about all his beloved children and gives them his care. He thinks of each of them as though he did not think of all the others. *(Francis de Sales)*

The ultimate personal relationship
In the Old Covenant people longed to speak to God face to face. However, fully satisfying this longing only became possible when Jesus said, 'The one who sees me sees the Father.' What was initiated when the Prophets experienced God calling them by name, has been expanded to an amazing degree now that we are called to relate with the Father just as Jesus does. 'And because you are children, God has sent the Spirit of his Son into our hearts, crying, "Abba! Father!"' (Gal 4:6)

The story of how the Spirit leads us into this consistently unique relationship is the story of our personal vocation. By getting in touch with this story and with how God has accepted and affirmed us over the years we can glimpse the way God sees us and who we are in his eyes. In this way we glimpse our deepest significance and we are invited to believe that we live within the family circle of the Trinity and share their glory. 'The glory that you have given me I have given them, so that they may be one, as we are one, I in them and you in me, that they may become completely one.' (Jn 17:22-23) In the intimate knowledge of this relationship the Spirit leads us into, we meet at the deepest level the two needs that Mario sought to meet in his relationship with Beatrice, the need for an intimate relationship in which our uniqueness is recognised and the need to find our true significance, the glory we are made for. (Ps 8)

> Each mortal thing does one thing and the same:
> Deals out that being indoors each one dwells;
> Selves – goes itself; myself it speaks and spells,
> Crying What I do is me: for that I came.
>
> I say more, the just man justices;
> Keeps grace: that keeps all his goings graces;
> Acts in God's eye what in God's eye he is –
> Christ. For Christ plays in ten thousand places,
> Lovely in limbs, and lovely in eyes not his
> To the Father through the features of men's faces.
> *(G. M. Hopkins)*

AN EXERCISE: Remember a person in your story who always made you feel important in the way he or she related with you. Relive an experience of this, noticing what the person said or did and what this meant to you. Let the person say this to you again in an imaginative way and notice how you feel about this. Take a scene in the gospel where Jesus relates with someone in a personal way, notice what Jesus says and then let him say these words to you a number of times until you feel comfortable with them.

Passionate Love

In one of Woody Allen's films called *Another Woman* we have the unfolding of the story of a woman's attitude to her passion, her feelings and her sexuality. At the beginning of the story we meet her as a successful lecturer in philosophy, very intellectual and controlled. She appears to be devoid of passion and shows little feeling apart from being embarrassed when her friends talk openly about their sex lives. When she tries to go further into the ivory tower of her intellectual life, by moving into an apartment to write a book, her intellectually dispassionate love is turned upside down.

As she gets down to work on her book she overhears a young woman in an adjoining apartment talking to her therapist. She is drawn into their conversation as it echoes her own experience. We watch her as she re-lives the memories aroused in her by what is happening next door. She gradually realises how stifling her feelings, for the sake of her intellectual pursuits, has led her to a loss of intimacy and authentic relationships.

Through going back to the memory of someone who had fallen in love with her, she learns to believe again in the possibilities in her own life of feeling and passion. As a result she experiences a sense of peace for the first time in many years and the creativity to write her book is released.

In the cherished memories life-story is love-story. *(Enda McDonagh)*

When two people fall in love they pass through a number of stages. Initially they experience each other as intensely attractive and are drawn to centre their lives on one another. They get to know as much as they can about each other and gradually want to change anything that might keep them apart. They want to find out if they are right for one another and if they love each other sufficiently to commit themselves to each other. Finally, they are ready for this permanent commitment.

> Nothing is more practical than finding God, that is, than falling in love in a quite absolute, final way. What you are in love with, what seizes your imagination, will affect everything. It will decide what will get you out of bed in the morning, what you do with your evenings, how you spend your weekends, what you read, whom you know, what breaks your heart, and what amazes you with joy and gratitude. Fall in love, stay in love, and it will decide everything. *(Pedro Arrupe S J)*

The effects of passionate love

A number of the effects of passionate love highlight how dramatically and deeply it influences our lives. What is initially most noticeable is the intensity of this love; the beloved assumes an attractiveness that makes him or her radiant, beautiful or glorious. This draws us towards the one we love so that we make him or her the centre of our life. This deep involvement engages our whole person, our body and its senses, our feelings and our intuition that glimpses the beauty and glory of the beloved. To become convinced of the love we glimpse or to believe in it involves a change in the way we see and feel about ourselves and the one we love, a change of mind and heart. The transforming power of passionate love is particularly good at bringing about this change. This is so in the early years of a relationship and on the long journey into making our relationship more and more permanent and profound.

> Sail forth – steer for the deep waters only.
> Reckless O Soul, exploring, I with thee, and thou with me,
> For we are bound where mariner has not yet dared to go,
> And we will risk the ship, ourselves and all.
> O my brave soul! O farther, farther sail!
> O daring joy, but safe! are they not all the seas of God!
> O farther, farther, farther sail! *(Walt Whitman)*

The transforming power of passionate love

While we identify passionate love with the relationship between a man and a woman and often with the physical-sexual side of this, passionate love is not confined to this relationship. Though the man-woman relationship is probably the best illustration of how passionate love develops and of its effects, this kind of love underlies all relationships. It is the essential energy urging us to realise our dream or the catalyst for the transformation of our mind and heart that our dream of love, intimacy and joy demands.

> The lesser gods are decorous
> And with a meek petition wait;
> But love comes, fixing his own hour,
> And hammers at the gate.

Passionate love can power the ongoing change of mind and heart necessary if our relationships are to become permanent and profound. As we continue to make these changes our relationships become more harmonious and quieter. This does not mean that the passion has gone out of them for as the film director, John Borman, says, 'passion is surely the becoming of a person'. The passionate life is but an expression of the urge of Eros to realise our dream.

The passionate life the Trinity inspire

Our human experience of passionate love is particularly significant in giving us a clear and engaging impression of the most important reality in the life of a Christian. This is the desire of the three persons of the Trinity to reveal how passionately they love each person. The passionate nature of God's love is seen in the Prophets and in the Song of Songs. There it is portrayed as the love of the bridegroom for his bride, of the Lover for the one in whom he delights. 'You shall be called My Delight Is in Her, and your land Married; for the Lord delights in you, and your land shall be married ... as the bridegroom rejoices over the bride, so shall your God rejoice over you.' (Is 62:4-5, Sg 8:7-8)

'To set the earth on fire'

From the beginning to the end of his life, Jesus is passionate about making the nature of his Father's love known to us; (Jn 1:18, 17:26) about making known that he and his Father love us just as they love each other. (Jn 15:9) He portrays his love as a burning fire with which he wants to set us on fire. 'I came to bring fire to the earth, and how I wish it were already kindled! I have a baptism with which to be baptised, and what stress I am under until it is completed!' (Lk 12:49) Jesus wants us to be on fire with this love, to 'abide in' it by receiving and returning it with our whole 'heart, soul, mind and strength'.

The love the Spirit leads us into is expressed by Jesus in what John and Paul see as the climax of God's passionate love for us: Jesus' love of us to 'the utmost extent'. (Jn 13:1) 'God's love has been poured into our hearts through the Holy Spirit ... God proves his love for us in that while we still were sinners Christ died for us ... For if while we were enemies, we were reconciled to God through the death of his Son, much more surely, having been reconciled, will we be saved by his life.' (Rom 5:5-10)

> 'Then said our good Lord Jesus Christ, 'Art thou well pleased that I suffered for thee?' I said, 'Yea, good Lord, I thank Thee; Yea good Lord, blessed may'st Thou be.' Then said Jesus our kind Lord: 'If thou art pleased, I am pleased: it is a joy, a bliss, and endless satisfying to me that ever suffered the Passion for Thee; and if I might suffer more, I would suffer more.' *(Julian of Norwich)*

AN EXERCISE: Take a piece of God's Word that portrays his passionate love for you, e.g. Hos 2:14-20 and after you have quietened and centred yourself, contemplate how God, Jesus, and the Spirit love you in this way. Then tell each in turn how you feel about what they have said to you. Do the same with the passionate nature of the three person's desire to reveal their love to you, e.g. Jn 16:13-15, 17:26. Finally, in light of Lk 10:25-28 or Jn 15:9-10 reflect on the passionate response they invite you to make to their love.

CHAPTER 37

Permanent Love

In his play, *Much Ado About Nothing*, Shakespeare focuses our attention on Beatrice and Benedick as they seek to be assured of each other's love. In public they maintain a facade of indifference to each other but in private they each strive desperately to ascertain the truth of the other's love. We are entertained as we see how being the object of one another's love is gradually moved from being peripheral to becoming the central passion of their lives. We notice how dependent they are on each other's positive regard and how exhilarated they become when they catch a glimpse of it. They are momentarily intoxicated by it but easily fall back again into unbelief. They need to hear this assurance of love again and again and even when they do hear it repeatedly their conviction does not grow and become strong enough to overcome the self-doubts they are prone to.

Like all good stories, *Much Ado About Nothing*, speaks to our dream. It invites us to appreciate how central to it is our conviction that the love of others is real and lasting. Like Beatrice and Benedick we have difficulty listening to the voices of those who accept and affirm us and even more so believing what they say.

In his book *Four Loves*, C. S. Lewis describes passionate love as the most impermanent of loves. So, we may ask, can it survive the ups and downs of any relationship and even grow? For example, is the promise that marriage makes to satisfy in a lasting way the hunger we are for love, intimacy and joy, a realistic one? That their love will last is certainly the heartfelt desire of each couple when they promise to be together till death parts them.

Is the wedding day dream unrealistic?
The dream people have on their wedding day is often not realised in the way they hope for. It sometimes ends in the sadness of

separation or offers only a modicum of the love, intimacy and joy it promised. Is this because they had not taken into account or learnt to live contentedly with their limitations and sinfulness? This side of themselves can either lead them to a growing closeness or to a 'creeping separateness'.

> One day in early Spring we thought we saw the answer. The killer of love is creeping separateness ... The failure of love might seem to be caused by hate or boredom or unfaithfulness with a lover; but these were the results. (*Sheldon Vanauken, A Severe Mercy*)

Cultivating a love that lasts

If we learn to accept our weakness and waywardness and those of the other, we do not become preoccupied with them. We can see this side of ourselves in perspective and see and appreciate the large percentage of ourselves that is gifted. When we cultivate the glimpses we get of our good qualities and make our own of these, they become convictions. These convictions about what is true and worthwhile accumulate to form a vision of goodness and beauty that leads to a series of positive feelings such as joy and gratitude. In this way the intense love, intimacy and joy of the early stages of being in love do not disappear but gradually become quieter as they deepen.

The reason why some relationships do not last is that they get stuck at the sensate and feeling levels. This is especially so if negative feelings are not dealt with and so come to dominate the relationship. These negative feelings create an emotional distance between ourselves and others and make it difficult to foster glimpses of goodness and beauty we are given. When these glimpses of our worth are not cultivated, our convictions about our significance for others are eroded and our belief in ourselves is diminished.

Can the intensity of love last?

It is an unfair expectation that any human being should be asked to satisfy the unlimited longing for a love that is unlimited. Only God can love us with a passion that endures all along the road we travel in life. 'The Lord your God, who goes before you, is the one who will fight for you, just as he did for you in Egypt before your very eyes, and in the wilderness, where you saw how the Lord your God carried you, just as one carries a child, all the way that you travelled until you reached this place. But in spite of this, you have no trust in the Lord your God, who goes before you on the way to seek out a place for you to camp, in fire by night, and in the cloud by day, to show you the route you should take.' (Deut 1:30-33)

The foundation of a love that lasts

The reason we can rely on the intensity of God's love enduring in spite of our waywardness is that we participate in the divine life. (2 Pet 1:4) We are loved by Jesus, the Father and their Spirit as they love each other, with a love that is everlasting. (Jn 15:9-10, Jer 31:3) In human relationships the intensity of the way we relate can be eroded or damaged by infidelity, neglect or indifference. It is, therefore, hard for us to believe that in spite of our infidelity the Father continues to see and love in us what he sees and loves in Jesus. (Jn 10:14)

> So great was your love
> that you gave us your Son as our redeemer.
> You sent him as one like ourselves,
> though free from sin,
> that you might see and love in us
> what you see and love in Christ.
> (Preface of Sundays VII)

The permanence of this passionate love God has for each of us is evident in many places in the Old and New Covenants. For example, Hosea assures us that God's love will never lose its intensity. No matter what, it will lure us into the desert to win our hearts anew. 'I will take you for my wife forever; I will take you for my wife in righteousness and in justice, in steadfast love, and in mercy. I will take you for my wife in faithfulness; and you shall know the Lord'. (Hs 2:19-20) In the way Jesus deals with Peter's betrayal we see how our infidelity once acknowledged, can lead to an even more intimate relationship. 'When they had finished breakfast, Jesus said to Simon Peter, "Simon son of John, do you love me more than these?" He said to him, "Yes, Lord; you know that I love you." Jesus said to him, "Feed my lambs".'(Jn 21:15) After the resurrection when Jesus gives us the gift of the Holy Spirit he sees her work among us as one of reconciling us to God and to each other. (Jn 20:22-23) In spite of our neglect of the Spirit's constant enlightenment and attraction, Jesus promises us that she will remain with us forever. 'And I will ask the Father, and he will give you another Advocate, to be with you forever.' (Jn 14:16) In one of his best known sonnets, Shakespeare highlights how integral to true love is its constancy, 'love is not love which alters when it alteration finds'.

> Let me not to the marriage of true minds
> Admit impediments, love is not love
> Which alters when it alteration finds,
> Or bends with the remover to remove;
> O no! it is an ever fixed mark
> That looks on tempests and is never shaken
> It is the star to every wand'ring bark,
> Whose worth's unknown, although his height be taken.
> Love's not Time's fool, though rosy lips and cheeks
> Within his bending sickle's come;
> Love alters not with his brief hours and weeks,
> But bears it out even to the edge of doom.
> If this be error and upon me proved,
> I never writ nor no man ever loved.
> *(William Shakespeare)*

AN EXERCISE: After quietening and centring yourself, enter a dialogue with the wayward companion you bring to the sacrament of reconciliation or with whom you say the Confiteor at the beginning of Mass. Give this wayward side of yourself a chance to speak and then respond to what it says. Let each of you say how you see and feel about what has happened between you and how this has influenced your image of each other. Say how you would like to see things work out between you in the future and what you both want to do about this. When you finish the dialogue, write down what has emerged from it.

Profound love

The film *Shadowlands* tells the story of how C. S. Lewis met and fell in love with Joy and how he coped with her death four years after they married. Because of the circumstances surrounding her final illness they were forced to face profound issues about their love for each other. When they first met they were both mature and articulate people and were able to express their experiences of their inner journey in a profound and engaging way. This was what moved people so much who saw this film.

We all want our relationships to deepen or become more profound. We want them to become intimate in the sense that we want to make known our inmost self to those we love. However, there is a high price to be paid for this as our relationships need a lot of time, effort and resources if we are to develop and deepen them. The pressures of work and rearing a family mean that we may not make room for this to happen; we may not be willing to make the space necessary to be alone and to go on 'the great psychic journey' we are all invited to undertake.

When it comes to the important things one is always alone … The way that one handles this absolute aloneness is the way in which one grows up, is the great psychic journey of everyman. *(May Sardon, Journal of a Solitude)*

Joseph Campbell, who spent his life studying folklore and the stories people tell, says in his book, *The Hero With a Thousand Faces*, that the basic theme of these stories is our inner journey. He finds that the object of this journey is to know the love of the mother-father God and the union and bliss this love draws us into.

There is only one journey. Going inside yourself. *(Rainer Maria Rilke)*

'Do this and you will live'

For the Bible the inner journey is our quest to realise all the potential of the image of God in which we are made. The Great Commandment clarifies how we do this by getting our whole person involved in the love we receive and return within the main relationships of our lives. For Jesus, keeping this commandment is what life is all about. He tells us 'Do this and you will live.' (Lk 10:25-28)

Jesus clarifies further the object of our inner journey in his commandment that we love others as he has loved us. (Jn 15:12) In this commandment Jesus focuses our attention on the vision he gives us of his love and on the interior knowledge of this love that the Spirit leads us into. Thus our inner journey becomes our lifelong effort to follow the path along which the Spirit leads us into 'all the truth' or into the love of the Father which Jesus expresses in human terms. (Jn 16:13) As we have seen, the Spirit leads us into this love by enlightening our minds and attracting our hearts and it is through reflection that we notice and name this enlightenment and through prayer that we savour and assimilate it. (Lk 8:15)

Love is as profound as what is shared

The depth of our love or how profound it becomes depends on how much of ourselves we are willing and able to share. In our day to day relationships we may share only our outer world even though with family and friends we may share something more. Any depth of sharing is difficult as it depends on our ability to be aware of and to appreciate what is going on within us. However, no matter how much we share it gives us but a fleeting glimpse of what Jesus wants to share with those who are willing to hear the word and 'take it to themselves and yield a harvest through their perseverance'. (Lk 8:15)

'All I have is yours!'

The profound nature of God's love is seen in his desire to reveal himself to us as far as we allow him to do so. His desire for intimacy, or to make known his inmost self, becomes clear in the words of the prophet Hosea: 'Therefore, I will now allure her, and bring her into the wilderness, and speak tenderly to her ...

And I will take you for my wife forever; I will take you for my wife in righteousness and in justice, in steadfast love, and in mercy. I will take you for my wife in faithfulness; and you shall know the Lord.' (Hos 2:14-20) Jeremiah tells us that in the new covenant God will write his covenant on the heart of each person: that God will communicate his love to the inmost part of each of us. 'But this is the covenant that I will make with the house of Israel after those days, says the Lord: I will put my law within them, and I will write it on their hearts; and I will be their God, and they shall be my people. No longer shall they teach one another, or say to each other, 'Know the Lord' for they shall all know me, from the least of them to the greatest.' (Jer 31:33-34)

> Gift better than himself God doth not know;
> Gift better than his God no man can see.
> This gift doth here the giver given bestow;
> Gift to this gift let each receiver be.
> God is my gift, himself he freely gave me;
> God's gift am I and none but God shall have me.
> (*Robert Southwell*)

The depth at which Jesus shares with us
Judging by the depth at which we normally share it is hard for us to believe that Jesus wants to share with us the depths of his inner world, his whole relationship with his Father, their love and its glory, their union and its joy. However, this is the world Jesus opens up to us in all its fullness and splendour, in chapters 14-17 of John's gospel.

The four levels at which we can share
How profound our love becomes depends not just on what we share but on the level at which we share this. For example, we might share at a sensate level by telling the story of an event in our life but we might also share the significance of this event if we have taken the pains to understand and articulate it. There is also the possibility of sharing at a profoundly personal level, our positive and negative feelings about the event. At the deepest level we might share our convictions about what is true and worthwhile for us.

Each of the levels at which we relate make an indispensable

contribution to the wisdom we share. Even though the most profound love is experienced in the conviction of being loved, unless this has its roots in our story, in the feelings and in the insights our story inspires, our convictions tend to become ideas and not the interior knowledge of being loved that engages our whole person.

Paul's prayer in his letter to the Ephesians describes how profound the love is that the Father, Jesus and the Spirit lead us into: 'I pray ... that you may be strengthened in your inner being with power through his Spirit ... to comprehend, with all the saints, the breadth and length and height and depth, and to know the love of Christ that surpasses knowledge, so that you may be filled with all the fullness of God.' (Eph 3:14-21) This is the love the Spirit pours into our hearts and leads us into so that we have an interior knowledge of it. Knowing that we are loved in this way means that we flower 'again from within'.

> ... sometimes it is necessary
> to reteach a thing its loveliness,
> ... and retell it in words and in touch
> it is lovely
> until it flowers again from within, of self-blessing;
> (Galway, St Francis and the Sow)

AN EXERCISE: Take some people you relate with in depth and notice what you share with each of them. Notice at what level you share, whether it is just information at a sensate level or whether you share your feelings, insights or convictions about what is true and worthwhile. Finally, enter a dialogue with Jesus and talk about what you share or would like to share with each other.

Joyful Love

There was once a mechanic who realised he was more than a mechanic as people came to consult him because they found him wise and courageous. So many flocked to where he worked that he had to give up his job to attend to the needs of those who wanted to avail of his wisdom. He told those who came to consult him that within us there is given the power to be rich or poor, to be a slave or free, to be healthy or sick, to be happy or unhappy and that it is we ourselves who control this power. When people failed to hear this and heaped responsibility for their lives on him he asked God to relieve him of this burden. God granted his request but asked him to deliver a final message to his followers. So he gathered the people together and asked them if they would be willing to do what God wanted, no matter what the price was. When they said they would, he told them, 'God commands you to be happy as long as you live'. At this the crowd was silent.

It has always puzzled me that even though happiness or joy is an essential part of the Bible's way of seeing things, we have such difficulty accepting this as central to what we believe. I grew up with the belief that happiness was something I should expect to find in the next life and only partially and intermittently here and now. Along the way I have slowly moved towards other convictions, rooted in Jesus' teaching in which our constant and complete happiness are inseparable from our faith in his love. The realisation of how important the constant and complete happiness of those I love is for me, and how important my happiness is for them, has helped me to adjust to the fact that our happiness is God's will. Surely God is at least as concerned for my happiness as my family and friends are for mine and I am for theirs.

The joy that is central to revelation
Even though we long for a happiness that is constant and complete, it seems an unrealistic ideal. However, even in the Old Covenant the prophet Jeremiah confirms the belief that God's will is our happiness or that God has a plan for our peace. (Jer 29:11) Joy is also central to Jesus' revelation of his Father's love: 'As the Father has loved me, so I have loved you; abide in my love. If you keep my commandments, you will abide in my love, just as I have kept my Father's commandments and abide in his love. I have said these things to you so that my joy may be in you and that your joy may be complete.' (Jn 15:9-11) The joy Jesus offers is a share in his own complete joy and it is also a constant joy or one that will never be taken away from us. 'I will see you again, and your hearts will rejoice, and no one will take your joy from you.' (Jn 16:20-22)

Joy has its deepest roots in our faith or in our conviction that we are loved by Jesus just as he is by his Father. (Jn 15:9-11) According to John of the Cross, another source of joy is our love for God. 'The soul of the one who loves God always swims in joy, always keeps holiday and is always in a mood for singing.' Nothing can come between us and the joy that God's love leads us into, neither the experience of our own human poverty in the form of our limitations and sinfulness nor our experience of the most extreme hardships. (Rom 8:35, Mt 5:1-12) 'As they left the council, they rejoiced that they were considered worthy to suffer dishonour for the sake of the name.' (Acts 5:41)

> The happiest heart that ever beat
> Was in some quiet breast,
> That found the common daylight sweet,
> And left to heaven the rest.

Joy pervades the Christian environment
As we learn to believe in Jesus' love our joy becomes a distinctive feature of the environment that this love creates and sustains for us. (Jn 16:20-22) We experience what this environment is like in the resurrection scenes in the gospels and especially in the profound commentary on these scenes that John gives us in chapters 14-17 of his gospel. We see what this means in practice in the Acts of the Apostles where joy pervades the atmosphere in

which Christians live. In the writings of Paul we see how the Christian community expands out beyond the Jewish world and that peace and joy 'in the Holy Spirit' are for Paul what distinguishes this community. 'For the kingdom of God is not food and drink but righteousness and peace and joy in the Holy Spirit.' (Rom 14:17) This 'peace and joy in the Holy Spirit' came to characterise the fulfilment of the Christian life in what Paul calls 'the fruit of the Spirit'. 'The fruit of the Spirit is love, joy, peace, patience, kindness, generosity, faithfulness, gentleness, and self-control. (Gal 5:22-23) Since the culture in which people live is shaped by the vision they adopt as their own and the feelings this gives rise to, the Christian culture, shaped as it is by the vision faith gives us, is characterised by the joy that springs from our faith. As a result, we are invited to be part of a culture where enjoyment is more important than concern.

If we are made for joy and to live in a culture in which the possibilities for joy are unlimited, we need to ask ourselves why we make excuses for not coming to the banquet. (Mt 22:1-14) Is it because cultivating this joy requires a lifelong effort to foster faith in Jesus' love that joy has its roots in? Another reason may be that we harbour the illusion that our happiness is controlled largely by forces outside ourselves. In fact, happiness is an inside job as it depends on the vision we adopt or on the way of seeing life that faith in Jesus' love provides.

> The foundation of content must spring up in a man's own mind and he who has so little knowledge of human nature as to seek happiness by changing everything but his own disposition, will waste his life in fruitless effort and multiply the grief which he purposes to remove. *(Samuel Johnston)*

Turning our mourning into dancing
When we fall victim to sadness and a loss of hope, Jesus has a deep desire to turn our mourning into dancing. (Ps 30:11-12) We see this desire being translated into action when Jesus meets two of his disciples on the road to Emmaus and leads them from sadness to joy and from despair to exuberant enthusiasm. (Lk 24) Through interpreting what has happened to them in the light of the love revealed in the Word and especially in the breaking of

bread, Jesus gives them a vision in which they see that 'Earth's crammed with heaven.'

> Earth's crammed with heaven,
> And every common bush afire with God.
> But only he who sees, takes off his shoes.
> The rest sit round it and pluck blackberries.
> *(E. B. Browning)*

Different levels of experience at which we find joy

Sobriety is the virtue that brings our joy to completion in that it cultivates a balance of the joys that come from the four levels at which we relate. (Lk 12:27, Lk 10:21, Mk 8:19-21, Mk 5:34, Jn 20:29) Each of these has its own distinctive joy. For example, there is the joy our body experiences through its senses as well the delight our heart experiences in a whole range of feelings, such as gratitude, joy and hope. Then there is the joy we get from our glimpses of being accepted, affirmed and being of significance in the lives of others. However, the deepest source of our joy comes from the conviction that we are loved by Jesus and his Father just as they love each other. (Jn 15:9-11)

> Up, heavy hearts, with joy your joy embrace.
> From death, from dark, from deafness, from despairs,
> That life, this light, this Word, this joy repairs.
> *(Robert Southwell)*

AN EXERCISE: Remember and record a few times in your life when you experienced a deep joy. What place does joy play in your life now? Would you like to strike a better balance between the time, energy and resources you make available to the joyful and the more serious side of yourself? Enter a dialogue with Jesus about the way you would like to establish a culture of enjoyment in your life. After the dialogue, outline on paper what you talked about.

PART 6

Introduction

The gospels can be seen as the story of how Jesus goes around making friends, leading those who believe in what he reveals to them into his own relationship with his Father. In this extraordinarily rich vision of friendship Jesus shares with us 'everything' he shares with his Father: their love, their glory, their union and their joy. The beauty of this vision is unfolded for us in chapters 14-17 of John's gospel.

By leading us into an interior knowledge of 'all the truth', or into an ever deeper appreciation of the love of God that Jesus embodies, the Spirit expands and deepens the friendship Jesus establishes with us. (Jn 16:13) In response we are asked to immerse our whole person in the love that Jesus reveals to us in the gospel stories and at Mass. We are invited to do this by means of an ongoing conversation in which we listen to and savour all that is revealed to us.

The chapters of Part 6 begin with one on the history of friendship. This centres on the magnificent view of friendship in the theology of Thomas Aquinas. Then there are four chapters devoted to Thomas' *three elements of friendship*. The first element, *benevolence*, is the essentially affirming attitude of Jesus in each gospel story where he initiates a friendship by making his Father's love known to us. The second element is that this benevolence is *mutual*, or a two-way relationship as we respond to Jesus' love by immersing our whole person, body, soul, mind and heart in it. The third element is the ongoing *conversation* necessary if we are to maintain our friendship by listening and responding to the word of God. The final chapter focuses on the union or distinctive kind of intimacy that friendship with Jesus brings about.

The three elements of friendship

'I have called you friends because I have told you everything
I have heard from the Father.' (Jn 15:15)

1 Benevolence: Adopting an affirming attitude
    Jesus shares the love he and the Father share

2 Mutual sharing: where both sides adopt this affirming attitude
    Jesus invites us to abide in his love

3 Conversation: friendship is maintained by ongoing dialogue
    Jesus asks us to listen to the word of God
    and to hold it fast

CHAPTER 40

A brief history of friendship

This brief history begins with how friendship was seen in pre-Christian times. Socrates saw it as our desire for the happiness of those we love but for him it was not necessary that this desire be mutual. Plato thought of friendship in terms of Eros and the role of this in our relationships as we make our way up out of the darkness of the cave into the light of day. Aristotle noticed that people based friendship on what was useful and pleasurable but for him only a friendship based on virtue was worthy of the name. He developed the notion of friendship as a mutual sharing of what people have and that true friendship is based on this. In this concept of friendship, what people share in their quest for each other's good can be knowledge, activity or enjoyment. Friendship in wishing another well takes for its measure a right self-love so that a friendship with another is like a friendship with oneself. For Aristotle friendship arose from nature more than from a need for pleasure or gain and friendship more than anything else aroused people to a better estimate of their own worth.

As Aristotle's writings did not become available in Europe until the 12th century, among early Christian writers Cicero's book *De Amacitia* was the most influential body of teaching on friendship. Cicero was an eclectic and drew on many sources for his definition of friendship. For him it was 'nothing else than an accord in all things, human and divine, conjoined with mutual good will and affection.' He had a very high estimation of friendship and apart from wisdom considered it the greatest gift.

Among the early Christian writers who spoke about friendship the most influential were Ambrose, Cassian and Augustine. Ambrose thought of friendship as the perfection of Christian love, while Cassian, who brought the wisdom of the desert fathers to the West, saw friendship as shared love or agape. For Augustine, friendship never became an important theological theme as in his experience it was too fickle and ambivalent. He thought of love as the basis of life and of central importance. Love for him was the love of God and all else was loved in as far as it led to God. This became the organising theme of Augustine's theology and marked the break between antiquity and the middle ages. Augustine's image of friendship, as two people walking side by side looking out at a common vision, has had a profound influence on our thoughts about friendship.

The middle ages

Friendship played a prominent role in many areas of life in the middle ages but in monastic life it was seen as distracting, problematic and a threat to communal harmony. Benedict, while being wary about friendship among the immature, left the way open for it between those who had reached maturity and especially between those monks and their abbot.

Two major influences: Aelred of Riveaux

The two most influential figures in the development of our ideas of Christian friendship were Aelred of Riveaux and Thomas Aquinas. Aelred, born in 1110, became a Cistercian and for the monks of his time the Song of Songs provided the language used to describe divine love. Aelred's thought was shaped more by the Word than by scholasticism and his knowledge of literary sources meant he represented the essence of Christian humanism in the twelfth century. While Augustine saw heaven as the place where we experience the fruition of love, Aelred thought it could be enjoyed in the here and now in a spiritual friendship.

Aelred felt that we, like the early Christians, are invited to be one in mind and heart and to share all. He also felt that this trusting and mutually confiding attitude pertained to the few whereas charity pertained to all. Aelred was unique in seeing friendship as the highest state on the way to perfection. He believed friends could open up each other's heart to God in a way that involved their whole person. Thus human friendship is valued by Aelred for its similarity with the friendship God desires with us. His originality lies in his conviction that our lives here and now afford an experience of eternal union, not only with God in prayer but with each other as well. Therefore, we must learn the wisdom of human friendship as it is valuable in providing us with a way to enter the divine friendship Jesus seeks with us. There has been a reluctance among Christians to give friendship the prominent position that Aelred gave it so that his teaching about friendship has, like that of St Thomas Aquinas, never been accepted.

Thomas Aquinas

Thomas Aquinas rests his mature teaching about friendship on Jn 15:15. Friendship is initiated by God's self-disclosure and because we belong to the body of Christ we are able to listen to and make our own of this. Thus we are able to share in the divine life, its love, union and joy. Thomas was deeply influenced by Aristotle's ideas on friendship and took three elements from his teaching as essential to friendship. The first element, *benevolence*, means God wants us to enjoy what he enjoys and equips us to do so. Thomas sees God as passionate about giving us a vision of himself as love and wanting us to enter the union and joy created and sustained by this love. To enter this union and the joy essential to it we must abide in or immerse our whole person in God's love. In this way the second element is put in place when we return God's love and it becomes *mutual*. Through ongoing *conversation*, as the third element of friendship, we expand and maintain it. Thomas sums up these elements of friendship as follows: 'Caritas signifies not only the love of God, but also a certain friendship with him, which implies besides love, the mutual return of love, together with a certain mutual communication.'

Most extraordinary about Thomas' idea of friendship is that he places it at the heart of Christianity; he writes: 'It seems that love is the same as friendship.' For Thomas, friendship is the quintessential model of Christian love and in the light of this it is a great mystery that something as beautiful as his teaching about friendship never took hold of the Christian imagination. It has never attained the role that the passionate love portrayed in the Song has attained. Even though Thomas gained universal recognition and became the 'official' theologian of the church, his voice on friendship was scarcely heard. It is a sad fact that after his time his ideas on friendship appear in the great spiritual writers only in a very watered down way. In the 17th century a division took place between friendship with God, with self and with others. The drift from Thomas' teaching was furthered by a return among Catholic writers like Fenelon to an adverse view of human friendship.

Among Anglican divines and reform preachers there is a more positive view of friendship. People like Jeremy Taylor make a strong connection between human and divine friendship and Taylor portrays marriage as in essence friendship. John Burnaby was the first theologian since Thomas to argue on a scholarly level for friendship as the quintessential model of Christian love.

Among theologians like Karl Barth the drift away from friendship as central to Christianity continued with his separation of friendship from charity. *Eros and Agape* is the title of a two-volume treatise written by the Swedish theologian Anders Nygren in the 1930s. Its conclusion that agape is the only truly Christian kind of love, and that eros turns us away from God has had a huge influence. This separation of friendship from charity / agape and the belief that charity is the only truly Christian love has led to C. S. Lewis' conclusion:

> Very few modern people think friendship even a love at all ... To the ancients, friendship seemed the happiest and most fully human of all loves, the crown of life and the school of virtue. The modern world in comparison ignores it. (*C. S. Lewis, Four Loves*)

With Pope Benedict XVI's reinstatement of eros as an expression of divine love in his *Deus Caritas Est*, is it time to restore friendship to the central place in Christianity that Thomas Aquinas gave it?

AN EXERCISE. Check through this brief history of the notion of friendship and write down the ideas about it that appeal to you. Arrange these in any way you find helpful so that a picture of friendship emerges that is attractive for you.

CHAPTER 41

Three elements of Christian friendship

Italian For Beginners is a Danish film about six people who come together each week for a class in Italian. Their lives gradually intertwine as they get to know each other and friendships gradually form between them. These develop further during a holiday together in Italy. Whereas at the beginning of the film they were all alone and at odds with life, now they are happy in each other's company and there is a radiance about them. This is particularly apparent in a striking scene when they meet for a meal after their return from their holiday. Andreas, the local pastor and member of the group, arranges the meal and in it there is a suggestion of the love, intimacy and joy of the eucharistic meal in which Jesus shares his whole self with us and thus nourishes our friendship with him.

There is something extra that the experience of friendship adds to that of affection and falling in love. It is like an extra layer of care that is added to that which we receive through affection and passionate love. Friendship forms an environment that is warm and non-threatening. In it we pick up a sense of acceptance, appreciation and of being significant, often by means of the weak and gifted sides of ourselves being accepted and affirmed by means of banter.

As we saw in the previous chapter the two people who stand out for their understanding of the powerful influence of friendship on our lives are Aelred of Riveaux and Thomas Aquinas. Aelred belonged to the pre-scholastic monastic tradition and developed a practical understanding of what friendship meant in monastic life. Thomas belonged to the more speculative tradition of scholasticism. He was unique in the importance he attached to friendship and in identifying Christian love or charity with it. He wrote: 'It seems that charity is the same as friendship because friendship is likened to the superabundance of love: they both show the characteristic of love at its greatest. Both love and friendship value the beloved at an inestimable price as though they were the dearest thing. Therefore Christian love is the same as friendship.' By comparison with this sublime view of friendship C. S. Lewis believes that 'very few modern people think friendship even a love at all'.

> Many people when they speak of their 'friends' mean only their companions. But it is not friendship in the sense I give to the word. By saying this I do not at all intend to disparage the merely clubable relation. We do not disparage silver by distinguishing it from gold ... Very few modern people think friendship even a love at all ... To the ancients, friendship seemed the happiest and most fully human of all loves; the crown of life and the school of virtue. The modern world in comparison ignores it. (C. S. Lewis)

One going around making friends

The gospels are the story of how Jesus goes around making friends, drawing them into his own extraordinary relationship with his Father. (Jn 15:15) In doing this he shares 'everything' about the life he and his Father enjoy: their love, their glory, their intimacy and their joy. (Jn 17) The extraordinary nature of this friendship that Jesus invites us into may seem too idealistic when we compare it with the ordinary level at which we relate with our friends and the limited amount of ourselves we share with them. Thus the friendship that Jesus offers us may seem too much for our mind and heart to hope for and may explain why Jesus' understanding of it and the way Thomas Aquinas explained this has rarely been taken seriously.

Three elements of friendship

There is a bond formed in all friendships and its strength is proportionate to three things: what is shared, the level at which this is shared and the quality of the sharing. These three correspond roughly to Thomas Aquinas' three elements of friendship: to its 'benevolence', to its being two-way or 'mutual' and to its being exercised through ongoing 'communication'.

The first element: Benevolence

A friendship is determined by what we share and we may confine this to information and ideas or we may share the personal details of our story. When we tell our own story or part of it to another we may in the process share much more of ourselves than we are aware of when we share the insights, the feelings, and even the deep convictions that our story reveals. However, underlying all we share is our desire to be affirmed by and our willingness to affirm the other in a way that is often implied more than directly expressed. This affirmation is the essential benevolence we look for in friendship and that Jesus expresses an extraordinary degree of when he says, 'I have called you friends, because I have made known to you everything that I have heard from my Father.' (Jn 15:15).

The second element: mutual benevolence

The love we are largely receivers of as children and givers of as parents we share as friends; we both want the best for each other, to say to each other, 'It is good that you are.' This mutual benevolence or affirmation leads to a sense of mutual significance or worth. The foundation for this capacity for mutual affirmation and recognition of worth was laid when we were made in the image of God. As such we are capable of a God-like love and of recognising and affirming the glory or the radiance of this love in ourselves and in others. God has 'crowned us with glory and beauty' in the sense that we can acknowledge the radiance of God's love in each other. (Ps 8)

It is on this foundation that our baptism builds so that we are now capable of knowing the Father's love and its radiance just as Jesus does. 'I know my own and my own know me, just as the Father knows me and I know the Father.' (Jn 10:14-15) Jesus can now befriend us in the sense that he can share with us 'everything' about his own relationship with his Father, their love and its radiance or glory, their union and its joy. (Jn 15:15) We are invited to share this wonderful reality with each other just as he has shared it with us. (Jn 15:12, Chapter 9)

Friends will still be travelling companions, but on a different kind of journey, Hence we picture lovers face to face but friends side by side, their eyes look ahead. *(Four Loves, C. S. Lewis)*

The third element: communication
This third element of friendship is communication and its importance can be gauged by the saying that 'A relationship is as good as the communication going on within it.' In practice, our friendships depend heavily on the quality of the sharing or of the listening and responding that goes on within them. The practical realisation of the first two elements of friendship depends on the willingness of friends to learn the difficult skills of listening and then of responding in an emotionally honest way to what they have heard. Jesus tells us that we fulfil our Christian potential or bear fruit, in proportion to our ability to listen and respond wholeheartedly to the word of God. 'But as for that in the good soil, these are the ones who, when they hear the word, hold it fast in an honest and good heart, and bear fruit with patient endurance.' (Lk 8:15)

In the school of life
many branches of knowledge are taught.
But the only philosophy
that amounts to anything after all,
is just the secret of making friends
(Henry van Dyke)

AN EXERCISE: Recall a friendship you enjoy with someone and dwell with the story of how it began, some of the key events in its development and where you are in it now. Next, look at it from the point of view of the three elements of friendship and notice what way each of the three is present. Finally, enter into a dialogue with your friend about how you see your friendship, what it means to you now and how you would like it to develop.

CHAPTER 42

The first element of friendship: Benevolence

The film *Three Colours: Red* is about an unlikely relationship that develops between Valentine, a student who works part-time as a model, and Joseph, a retired judge. She is young, positive and caring while he is elderly, cynical and uncaring. Much is revealed in an opening scene when Valentine, driving home one dark night, runs into a dog and instead of driving on she goes to endless trouble to look after the dog. When she brings it back to its owner, Joseph, a relationship develops between them in which he is gradually drawn out of his small, sad world by her caring and yet challenging attitude towards him. Though they live in very different worlds they gradually learn to accept the flawed elements in each other's story as well as to appreciate all the goodness and glory they find there.

This film is a beautiful symbol of the first element of friendship. This is the *benevolence* that wants the best for our friends, that they would realise their dream. We want our friends to live in an environment where they are accepted and affirmed and that believing in this that they would grow in a sense of their unique significance. Central to the benevolence that is at the core of friendship is affirmation that, as we have seen in chapter 32, acceptance opens the door to and that, as we have seen in chapter 35, a sense of significance is the fruit of.

Without affirmation, love does not exist. Permeated with a proper attitude concerning the value of a person – and such an attitude we term affirmation – love reaches its fullness. Without this affirmation of the value of a person as a whole, love disintegrates, and in fact, does not exist at all. *(Karol Wojtyla)*

To make our own of the affirmation we receive from friends we need first to accept their acceptance of our limitations and sinfulness. If we do not, we will resist their affirmation because our sense of inadequacy will loom so large in our vision of ourselves that it will block our acceptance of what friends ask us to believe about ourselves. If, however, we learn to believe in their affirmation of us, a sense of our unique significance or importance will grow. We will then be able to take the risk of revealing ourselves to them, of spreading something as delicate as our dream of love and its beauty under their feet.

> But I, being poor, have only my dreams;
> I have spread my dreams under your feet;
> Tread softly because you tread on my dreams.
> (William Butler Yeats)

Our friends give us an impression of our importance for them by the way they relate with, look at and treat us. While we are adept at picking up negative messages, we leave most of what is positive or affirming unnoticed and unnamed. When we remain unaware of the ways our friends accept and affirm us, we are not nourished by the love they offer us and want us to take to heart.

> Nothing makes so much impression on the heart of man as the voice of friendship when it is really known to be such; for we are aware that it never speaks to us except for our advantage. (Rousseau)

One of the reasons we do not hear the positive things people say to us is that generally they are said in an indirect way. Most of the affirmation we receive is conveyed to us by what people do rather than by what they say. As a result, we can miss how much we mean to our friends unless we take time to notice the indirect ways they say this. As well as noticing the glimpses of our true self that friends give us, we need to name or articulate these glimpses if we are to understand and appreciate their significance. We are also called to go on the long journey towards belief in the various ways our friends accept, affirm and give us a sense of our true significance. This is a long and difficult journey for it involves a change of mind and heart, a change in the way we see and feel about ourselves.

How Jesus makes us his friends

As Jesus goes around making friends it is obvious that his priority is to affirm those he meets or to tell them the good news. (Mk 1:14-15) As we have already seen, we are inclined to think of and to treat this good news of God's love and providence in our lives primarily as concern and desire while in fact it is primarily appreciation and delight. We see this in the story of Zacchaeus where Jesus acknowledges his true significance by focusing his full attention on him. Jesus celebrates the fact that Zacchaeus is 'a son of Abraham' by sharing a meal with him in his house. In his encounter with Jesus, Zacchaeus is given a vision of Jesus' love, its radiance or glory and in this way a vision of his own radiance or glory. This vision of Jesus and of himself in Jesus' eyes obviously captivates and enraptures Zacchaeus, giving him an intense joy in who he is in Jesus' eyes and enthusiasm for all he may be. (Lk 19:1-10)

Friendship as a share in the life of the Trinity

Our baptism enables us to see this inspiring vision of Jesus and of ourselves and to be enraptured by it as Zacchaeus was. 'For in the one Spirit we were all baptised into one body ... and we were all made to drink of one Spirit.' (1 Cor 12:12-13) Through baptism we participate in the life of the Trinity and are led by the Holy Spirit into an intimate knowledge of their love and the fellowship that the radiance of this love draws us into. 'For all who are led by the Spirit of God are children of God. For you ... have received a spirit of adoption. When we cry, "Abba! Father!" it is that very Spirit bearing witness with our spirit that we are children of God, and if children, then heirs, heirs of God and joint heirs with Christ – if, in fact, we suffer with him so that we may also be glorified with him.' (Rom 8:14-17) Thus we are *in* the one who is glorified so that 'the Father sees and loves in us what he sees and loves in Christ.' (Preface for Sundays) It is hard to believe it but we are *in* the one in whom the Father delights. In light of our being joint heirs with Christ and 'glorified with him' we can see that the foundation has been laid for our friendship with Jesus, for sharing in everything he has and is in his relationship with his Father. 'I call you friends, because I have made known to you everything I have learnt from my Father.' (Jn 15:15) It is because of this that the prayer we say at the end of the spiritual exercises is so poignant:

I will ponder with much affection how much God our Lord has done for me, and how much he has given me of what he has, and finally, how much, as far as he can, the same Lord desires to give Himself to me according to his divine plan. (*The Spiritual Exercises*, No 234)

We can now see how accurate it is to describe the gospels as the story of how Jesus goes around making friends, in that he leads all who believe what he says into his own relationship with his Father. It is the Spirit who leads us into an interior knowledge of this reality. (Jn 16:13-15)

The light of love shines over all;
Of love that says, not mine and thine,
But ours, for ours is thine and mine.

AN EXERCISE: Tell the story of your friendship with Jesus by jotting down some key events in its development. What is the most important aspect of this friendship for you? Next, enter into a dialogue with Jesus about your friendship and write down what each of you say. Read the story of Jesus' meeting with Zacchaeus in Lk 19:1-10. In the story notice a way Jesus befriends Zacchaeus and then let him befriend you in this way. Tell him how you feel about this. Finally, reflect on the fact that it is the Spirit who guides you in prayer and then talk together about what you saw and felt in the exercise and how this was largely the Spirit's work in you.

CHAPTER 43

The second element of friendship: Mutual sharing

The film *Scent of a Woman* centres on two people, Frank, a middle aged retired colonel who is blind, and Charlie, a university student. Their paths cross when Charlie is employed to look after Frank over a long weekend when those who normally care for him take a break. Frank is so frustrated by his blindness that he plans to travel to New York to commit suicide. Not knowing Frank's plans, Charlie agrees to accompany him. Initially, Frank seeks to control their conversation but then gradually begins to listen to Charlie's story and to tell him his own. In the dialogue that ensues Frank gets a chance to work through his anger and this releases a capacity he has to pick up the scent of where people are and a capacity to respond to them in a charming way. We see an example of this at the end of the film when Frank returns to his young married relatives who care for him. Their two young children had been afraid of Frank because of his threatening way of relating with them. Now we see him engaging them, tuning in to where they are and drawing them out so that they are able to be themselves with him. Frank, whose life had been dominated by an anger that pushed people away, now reveals a capacity to befriend those he meets.

In this film we see a second element of friendship emerging when benevolence becomes mutual. When Frank and Charlie become sensitive and responsive to each other's inner world of relationships they become capable of and want to share this with each other.

Love consists in a mutual sharing of goods, for example, the lover gives and shares with the beloved what he possesses, or something of that which he has or is able to give;

and vice versa, the beloved shares with the lover. Hence if one has knowledge, he shares it with the one who does not possess it; and so also if one has honours, or riches. Thus, one always gives to the other. (No 231, *The Spiritual Exercises*)

It is as if we live in a house with a perimeter fence around it. We may allow a large number of people inside this fence but fewer into the house and fewer still into our inner room. This room represents our personal life, our experience of significant events and relationships and all we have learned from these about love and the dream it inspires. However, for various reasons most of this experience is not ours to share as it lies dormant.

We are reluctant to arouse our dormant experience because this would involve a risk as well as a lot of hard work and we baulk at both. The risk is that if we reveal ourselves to others they may not like what they see, the hard work is that involved in coming to know ourselves so that we might make ourselves known to others. In spite of our reluctance to arouse our dormant experience, we have a deep desire to be known and loved by others. Our friends are the ones most likely to satisfy this need for they provide a safe and an affirming environment in which to reveal our inmost self. By their affirmation they give us a vision of our true selves and ask us to believe in it. It is when, through reflection, we become aware of this vision and are willing to share it that we become friends and not just companions.

It is when two such persons discover, when, whether with immense difficulties and semi-articulate fumblings or with what would seem to us amazing and elliptical speed, they share their vision – it is then that friendship is born. (C. S. Lewis, *Four Loves*)

The benefits of sharing our vision
We are greatly helped on our journey into the mutual benevolence friendship requires if we make a habit of sharing our experience with a soul friend. In this affirming environment we have permission to share what lies below the surface of life and putting words on our experience of this helps us to understand it and appreciate its value. This mutual sharing essential to

friendship helps to discern our convictions of what is true and worthwhile and to clarify our inner wisdom that otherwise remains dormant. However, if this sharing is to be really beneficial, each person must be prepared to listen with sensitivity and respect, to draw each other out and only then to respond in an emotionally honest way to what the other has said.

The sharing in depth that Jesus calls for
The mutual sharing essential to the friendship Jesus calls us into is rooted in two major movements. The first movement is of God coming down the ladder stretching between heaven and earth to give us a gift of himself in complete self-disclosure and thereby to initiate a friendship with us. (Gen 28:12) The second is our movement up the ladder to God as we gradually learn to respond to God's love in an emotionally honest way. These two movements are epitomised in the Great Commandment in which we are called to be loved and to love in return with our whole person, body and soul, mind and heart. By involving our whole person in listening and responding to God's love we answer Jesus' call to 'abide in' his love. 'As the Father has loved me, so I have loved you; abide in my love. If you keep my commandments, you will abide in my love, just as I have kept my Father's commandments and abide in his love. (Jn 15:9-11, Lk 10:25-28) Thus our response to the friendship God initiates by revealing himself to us takes the form of a complete surrender of our heart to God.

> Dear Lord, I'll fetch Thee hence, I have a room –
> 'Tis poor, but 'tis my best – if Thou wilt come
> Within so small a cell, where I would fain
> Mine and the world's Redeemer entertain,
> I mean my heart. *(Anonymous)*

In offering God our 'heart' we are offering to get our whole person involved in sharing the vision the Trinity give us of 'everything' they have and are, their love, glory, union and joy. For our part we are invited to 'know the gift of God', (Jn 4:10) to gradually become aware of its extent and depth, to walk around in, to savour it, to say how we feel about it and to appropriate or believe in it. This is what is involved in the mutual affirmation of the second element of friendship when we say of God, 'My Beloved is mine and I am his'. (Sg 2:16, Jer 31:33)

Arcadia
My true love hath my heart, and I have his,
By just exchange, one for the other giv'n.
I hold his dear, and mine he cannot miss:
There never was a better bargain driv'n.

His heart in me, keeps me and him in one,
My heart in him, his thoughts and senses guides:
He loves my heart, for once it was his own:
I cherish his, because in me it hides.

His heart his wound received from my sight:
My heart was wounded with his wounded heart,
For as from me, on him his hurt did light,
So still methought in me his hurt did smart;
Both equal hurt, in this change sought our bliss:
My true love hath my heart and I have his.
(Sir Philip Sidney)

AN EXERCISE: Choose three friends and notice how much of this second element of friendship is part of your relationship with them. What do you share with each one? Is the sharing one-sided with any of them? Does each one listen to what you share and then draw you out? Notice how much each shares with you and if you are willing listen and to draw him or her out. Are you emotionally honest in your responses to what you reveal of yourselves to each other?

The third element of friend... Conversation

Cast Away is a film about a man called Chuck who found himself washed up on a small pacific island after the airline he was travelling on crashed. Initially, he was overcome by the solitude and at the mercy of the constant chatter of his emotions. When he settled down in his new home he painted a face on a football that had been washed up with him and began a conversation with an imaginary figure he called Malcolm that this face represented. This satisfied his need to say how he thought and felt about his situation and as time went on he was also able to hear what Malcolm wanted to say to him in reply. Through articulating his thoughts and feelings in this way he came to view his situation differently and rose to its challenge. It was as if he needed to converse in order to overcome his sense of being alone. By expressing what he thought and felt, he began to relate with himself in a way that previously he had been too busy to do. Through his conversations with Malcolm he was gradually able to befriend areas of himself from which he had previously been estranged.

Talking with ourselves

The conversations between Chuck and Malcolm are very like those which Ira Progoff in his *Intensive Journal* asks us to engage in through what he calls 'dialogues'. By means of these Progoff wants us to establish healthy relationships with areas of our life from which we have become estranged. For example, to befriend our body, Progoff advises us to recall some stages in the story of our relationship with it and then to say how we see and feel about our body now. He then asks us to say something to our body and let it reply and to continue this conversation until we have both said all we want to.

...ɪese 'dialogues' are surprised at how effec-
...ɔefriending areas of their lives with which they
...ɪtact. Conversation plays an essential role in the de-
...ʌent of all our relationships and especially that of friend-
...p. In practice, the development of the first two elements of
friendship depends on this third element of ongoing communication. The listening and responding involved in this plays a key
role in keeping us in touch with the affirmation of our friends.
To get by in life we may not need a great amount of this affirmation at any one time but we do need a constant supply of it.
This is because of the constant erosion of our experience of being
loved, caused by our tendency to give too much attention to our
limited or defective side so that this side often dominates our
vision of ourselves. By learning to communicate with both the
negative and the positive sides of life we remain in touch with
our true self and that of others. The alternative is to allow a wall
to be built that separates us from others.

The Wall

Some time between their first child and their last they allowed a wall to emerge between them. At the beginning it
was little differences that were not sorted out, unresolved
issues that were stored away. He hid his fear of failure
and she hid her sadness at losing him. Each sought refuge
in other places or persons, he sought solace in his work
while she channelled her energy into relating with their
children. So there it stood between them, so tall and thick
that they could no longer touch each other. It was not the
fruit of hostility or conflict so much as the creeping separateness that a failure to cultivate the art of conversation
leads to.

The art of conversation

To prevent a wall emerging between ourselves and our friends
we need to develop the art of conversation, the skill of listening
and responding effectively to each other. This is a difficult art to
learn as we tend to talk more than listen and, what is worse, to
talk without having listened.

We need to learn the skill of listening and of drawing each

other out. What we need to listen to is not so much each other's ideas as the insights we glean from what the other person says and the intimations they give us of how they feel. Drawing each other out involves highlighting what we have heard the other say and their feelings about this. We give our friends a great gift when we listen to them but no less a gift when we say honestly what we think and feel about what they reveal of themselves to us. Friendship is essentially affirming, and saying the goodness and the glory we find in each other is central to this affirming thrust. (cf chapter 9) This kind of listening and responding to each other encourages reflection in that it gives us the incentive to notice and name the positive and negative things going on within us. Sharing these means our friendship grows.

A Poison Tree
I was angry with my friend;
I told my wrath, my wrath did end.
I was angry with my foe;
I told it not, my wrath did grow. *(William Blake)*

Prayer as conversation with God
Since St Augustine's time, prayer has been seen as a conversation with God and the Benedictine method of prayer, which has had a powerful influence on our ways of praying, confirms this view. The fact that prayer is a conversation is rooted in God's desire to reveal himself to us, and engaging in the conversation this revelation calls for has always been seen as the most effective and practical way of answering Jesus' basic call to 'repent and believe the good news.' (Mk 1:14-15)

A major influence on seeing prayer as conversation has been the story of Jacob's dream in which he saw a ladder stretching between heaven and earth. The angels Jacob saw descending and ascending this ladder have, from earliest Christian times, become a symbol of our response to God's desire to converse with us. The meaning of this symbol is clarified for us when we are told that 'The Lord used to speak to Moses face to face, as one speaks to a friend.' (Ex 33:11) John gives this symbol of the ladder added depth when he reports the words of Jesus: 'Very truly, I tell you, you will see heaven opened and the angels of God ascending and descending upon the Son of Man. (Jn 1:51)

In the parable of the sower, Jesus calls us into this conversation when he invites us to listen and respond to the word of God: 'As for that in the good soil, these are the ones who, when they hear the word, hold it fast in an honest and good heart, and bear fruit with patient endurance.' (Lk 8:15)

We have already seen how the Spirit leads us into prayer by enlightening and attracting us. By enlightening us the Spirit highlights some aspect of Jesus' love and by attracting us the Spirit highlights the beauty of Jesus' love and thereby draws us towards making our own of it. For example, when we contemplate a gospel story the Spirit gives us a glimpse of some aspect of Jesus' love and invites us to be receptive to this by allowing Jesus to say to us what he is saying to someone in the gospel story. The Spirit also highlights the attractiveness of Jesus' love as it is portrayed in the gospel story we are contemplating. This attraction evokes a twofold response. The first involves expressing the feelings Jesus' love arouses within us and the second involves making our own of Jesus' love.

> The heart's dialogue with God
> Was his life's theme and he
> Explored the depths assiduously
> And without rest.
> (B Kennelly, *In memory of Patrick Kavanagh*)

AN EXERCISE: Recall a few people whose conversation you enjoy. Relive an experience in which one of them listened carefully to what you had to say and then relive an experience in which one responded honestly to what you had to say. Read the story in Luke 24 where Jesus listens and responds honestly to two of his disciples and then let Jesus listen and respond to what you wish to say to him. After you have done this reflect on whether you allowed Jesus to be as sensitive and responsive to you as the people are whose conversation you enjoy.

CHAPTER 45

The union that friendship creates and maintains

The Secret Garden is a film about Mary, a young girl who loses both her parents and is sent to live with her uncle in a big rambling house in a remote part of the country. Each day she is sent out by herself to play in the extensive grounds surrounding the house. Then one day she discovers the entrance to a secret garden and, even though it is a desolate place, having been neglected for many years, it becomes her favourite place to play. With the coming of spring and a certain amount of cultivation, the garden becomes beautiful and a place where she invites other young people to join her. Before she found her secret garden, she felt neglected, lonely and sad but now she feels loved by her friends and as a result she is happy. At the end of the film she expresses her belief that each of us is responsible for finding and cultivating our own secret garden or the environment in which we choose to live. 'The secret garden is always open now, open, awake and alive. If you look the right way, you can see that the whole world is a secret garden.'

God's secret Garden

The secret garden Mary found and cultivated symbolises the 'holding environment' each of us is responsible for finding and cultivating. This environment is a network of relationships with God, ourselves, others and the whole of creation. Initially, our environment is shaped by the affection we receive within our family but a quite different environment is formed when we fall in love. This environment develops still further as the passionate love which forms it becomes more and more permanent and profound and develops into the friendship described in the last three chapters. As our love develops in this way our environment becomes the product of a love that is 'as strong as death' or of 'a passion fierce as the grave'. 'Set me as a seal upon your heart, as a seal upon your arm; for love is strong as death, passion fierce as the grave. Its flashes are flashes of fire, a raging flame. Many waters cannot quench love, neither can floods drown it. If one offered for love all the wealth of one's house, it would be utterly scorned. (Sg 8:6-7)

The union friendship draws us into

For Jesus, friendship is the ultimate holding environment. It is based on what he shares with us and on how fully engaged he wishes us to become in all he shares. What Jesus wants to share, through his Spirit, is an interior knowledge of every aspect of the life he enjoys with his Father. He wants to share 'all the fullness of God', (Eph 3:19) to share 'everything' he shares with his Father – their love, glory, intimacy and joy. (Jn 17:13, 22-23) It is this complete self-revelation that makes us his friends. 'I have called you friends, because I have made known to you everything that I have heard from my Father.' (Jn 15:15)

That we might enter fully into this friendship, Jesus urges us to 'abide in' his love, to immerse our whole person 'heart and soul and mind and strength' in it and in the dream it inspires. (Jn 15:9-10, Lk 10:25-28) To help us abide in this love Jesus sends his Spirit to lead us step by step into it. The radiance of this love draws us into union with God and into the joy of this. (1 Jn 4:8-10, Jn 16:13-15) To get a fuller picture of the friendship that the three persons calls us into we will look at the love, the glory, the union and the joy that characterise it. We looked at these four in detail in the early chapters of this book so we will recall only the main features of them here.

The love we share

What makes us friends of Jesus is his sharing with us of 'everything' he and his Father share, which is essentially their love. (Jn 15:15) He spent his whole life making friends by revealing this love to all he met. 'I made your name known to them, and I will make it known (through sending the Spirit), so that the love with which you have loved me may be in them, and I in them.' (Jn 17:26) The Spirit continues this work of Jesus by leading us into the love she has poured into our hearts. As a result, we know the love Jesus and his Father share from the inside, or we are given an interior knowledge of it. (Rom 5:5, Jn 16:13-15)

The splendour of this love

A second aspect of the friendship Jesus draws us into is its glory. This is like a radiance, warmth or glow we notice when we reflect on the love of friends. This radiance was seen on the face of Moses after he had been speaking with God on the mountain. Paul says: 'His face was alight with heavenly splendour.' We see this glory in the gospel stories in the way Jesus relates with and loves people. He leads people to see his glory and also to see their own. (Jn 2:11, Lk 19:1-11, Jn 17:22) The Spirit, who enlightens and leads us into Jesus' love, reveals its attractiveness or glory in Jesus and in us too. 'We are transfigured in ever-increasing splendour into his image, and the transformation comes from the Lord who is the Spirit.' (2 Cor 3:18)

The union love draws us into

A third aspect of friendship Jesus draws us into is the intimacy, union or fellowship our being 'in Christ' leads to. This is the 'complete' union that the glory or radiance of Jesus' love draws us into in each gospel story but especially when he is 'lifted up' on the cross and in the glory of the resurrection. 'And I, when I am lifted up from the earth, will draw all people (all things) to myself.' (Jn 12:32, Jn 17:22-23) The Spirit gives us an intimate experience of what it means to be 'in Christ' before the Father, so that we can say with Jesus, 'Abba! Father!' 'God has sent the Spirit of his Son into our hearts, crying, "Abba! Father!"' (Gal 4:6)

The joy at the heart of friendship

A fourth aspect of the friendship Jesus draws us into is the joy that is central to it. This joy, which Jesus wants to be 'complete', is central to God's self-revelation and is even the purpose of it. 'As the Father has loved me, so I have loved you; abide in my love ... I have said these things to you so that my joy may be in you and that your joy may be complete.' (Jn 15:9-11) The 'complete' happiness Jesus wants us to enjoy is dependent on our abiding in his love or on our immersing our whole person in it as 'keeping the commandments' involves. (Jn 15:10) Paul also sees 'peace and joy in the Holy Spirit' as central to the kingdom of God or to the fellowship the Spirit cultivates. 'For the kingdom of God is not food and drink but righteousness and peace and joy in the Holy Spirit.' (Rom 14:17)

How Jesus leads us into this friendship
Reflection and prayer are the way in practice the Spirit uses to draw us into friendship with Jesus. Through reflection the Spirit invites us to notice some aspect of Jesus' love revealed, for example, in a gospel story. We are then invited through prayer to contemplate this love, to let its attractiveness grow and involve us as fully as possible. We can increase this involvement in our relationship with Jesus by letting him say to us the love he expresses for someone in the gospel story. Listening to Jesus expressing his love in this way stimulates feelings, such as joy, and by expressing these feelings we grow in intimacy with him. The growth of our friendship with Jesus depends a lot on our willingness to get engaged in conversations like this with him. In allowing him to reveal himself to us in this way Jesus can continue his work of making us his friends and drawing us into his own friendship with the Father and into the fellowship of their Spirit.

> From quiet homes and first beginning,
> Out to the undiscovered ends,
> There's nothing worth the wear of winning,
> But laughter and the love of friends. *(Hilaire Belloc)*

AN EXERCISE: After quietening yourself, read Jn 21:1-14 and dwell with one aspect of the way Jesus relates with his disciples. Spend some time letting the attractiveness of the love with which Jesus relates grow. Put words on what you hear Jesus saying to someone in the story and then let Jesus say these words to you a number of times so that you may savour them. Finally, tell Jesus how you feel about him saying these words to you. When you have finished this exercise write down what aspect of Jesus' love you focused on, how you let Jesus say this love to you and how this made you feel.